Spiritual

Growth

Peace in the Storm

By

Deirdre Kelley

authorHOUSE™

1663 LIBERTY DRIVE, SUITE 200
BLOOMINGTON, INDIANA 47403
(800) 839-8640
WWW.AUTHORHOUSE.COM

First published by AuthorHouse 05/10/05

ISBN: 1-4208-2980-7 (sc)

Printed in the United States of America
Bloomington, Indiana

This book is printed on acid-free paper.

2183

Chapter One

She couldn't exactly say it was a wrong choice and she couldn't say it was the right choice. And it was hard to think that it was a good choice that had simply gone wrong. What she could say was that it was a choice that ended very wrong. While she could pretty much conclude at what point she had first noticed something was wrong, she probably would never know exactly what happened. At best she would only be able to make guesses and surmises based on the actions of the other party. But regardless of what she endured on a daily basis, she had been determined to make the best of a bad situation as was within her power. There was just too much she could not overcome. And she had lost the battle. Now it was time to pick up the pieces and began again, and hopefully do it right this time.

As she walked away from the courthouse, she knew life would be vastly different from here on out. But she was much wiser then when she started on this journey. The divorce was final and he was moving on. She had to do the same, although alone. Well, not alone. She had the children who would be moving on with her.

As she drove toward home, Amy let her mind wander back to the beginning of her marriage. In the days that had preceded their marriage, Amy had not seen any of the tell-tale signs that she had been warned about by her friends. They told tales of his going out with other women while she finished school, alcoholic parties with his wild friends and a fierce temper when he did not get his way. But she saw none of that, either because she was "in love" or he had hidden it well. She had asked him about the rumors but he had denied them, saying her friends were trying to break them up. Brandon had been attentive, caring and patient even during the many wedding plans. Even when things went wrong, he showed her support in every way. Her friends admitted that perhaps they had been wrong about him or that he truly loved her and was willing to change his "evil" ways, as one friend had put it.

After the wedding things continued to run smoothly, with no signs of his harsh temper or his womanizing ways she had heard so much about. After Marshall came along a couple of years later, she noticed him staying at work longer but thought nothing about it. He had after all received a promotion and she felt that perhaps he had more responsibilities that demanded more of his time. By the time Sean was born, she no longer thought about his absence in the home, it was just the way it was. But when he was there, she began to witness the temper she had been warned about. It was often explosive, frightening her and the boys but was also short lived. There were always apologies and promises after the explosion. She began to be thankful for his absences.

As Amy got closer to home, her thoughts turned to the boys and what they had to go through before it was over. She had tried to keep peace in the house, to keep Brandon happy and the boys out of the way. Sometimes it did not matter what she did, it was not enough and the boys fell victim to their father's angry outbursts. She had tried to encourage the boys to love their dad even in the midst of the anger. Thinking of the children made her stomach tighten.

She knew it was going to be difficult for them growing up without a father. Not that he had been a large part of their lives, joining in their activities or attending any functions, but because of the stigma and the reduction of income they would all have to face. Her friends said not to count him out, but she didn't think he would be part of their lives much, if any. He had already made plans that did not include the children. And his current girlfriend, figuring highly in his plans, encouraged his separation from them.

Perhaps that was for the best, considering the lifestyle he had chosen and the destruction he had left behind. Amy didn't know what all he was involved with, or who all, but she certainly didn't want her children growing up thinking his life style was acceptable. She hoped her sons would prove to be more respectable and responsible adults. The burden of raising them to be as she desired would fall solely on her. It was going to be her life, her teaching, that would ultimately shape them to be the adults she hoped they'd be. She only hoped it was not too late to teach them the right way to live and treat people.

The boys would be coming home from school shortly. She knew they'd be curious about the day in court and she was unsure of what to tell them. She had already told them that she and their dad were getting a divorce, that he would no longer be living in the house. Somewhat sadly, they were not upset over his leaving. That reflected much on how they felt about him. It was not too surprising that they were not upset, though, with all his angry tantrums and his frequent absences from the house that went beyond working late. He was always angry about something and yelled at the closest person. She knew his job was stressful but he had anger that went beyond a bad day at work. It was not until after she had learned of the affairs and drug use that his anger turned physical. Hopefully, the boys did not know about the hitting, and no one knew about the drugs. But with any luck that was all in the past now.

Before she pulled into her driveway, she saw her mother's car. She grew more appreciative of her mother during the separation and divorce proceedings. She was always near to help around the house and with the boys. She gave a supportive shoulder to lean and cry on. She was not sure she could have went through all she did if not for her mother's strength. That had not always been so in the past. Amy knew her mother's disapproval of her marriage, or at least of her choice of mates. But then they had not been real close at that time. Their relationship didn't really develop until the boys came along. She often thought about what had happened in her mother's life that created a gulf between her and her mother before they had an opportunity to bond. But now she was grateful she and her mother had established a good relationship. Her mother would require a full explanation of what had happened in court. There was an hour before the boys came home so she would have time to give her a few details she did not want the boys to hear.

"Well, how did it go? Are you alright? Did he say anything to you? Was she with him?" her mother asked, greeting her at the door.

"Mother, let me get in the door before you bombard me with all those questions," she said, plopping down in a chair. "I guess things went okay. I've never gotten a divorce before so I don't really have anything to compare it to. But based on some of the things I saw going on with other couples getting a divorce, I'd have to say it went well. There was one couple there that was screaming and cursing at each other the whole time they stood in front of the judge. He told them if they didn't stop yelling he was going to put them in jail. If their marriage was anything like their divorce, it was really bad.

"But to answer your other questions, he really didn't say anything. The details were all worked out before we went to court so there wasn't really anything for either of us to say. And yes she was there. You know I kind of feel sorry for him."

"What do you mean you feel sorry for him? Why would you say that after the way he treated you? He completely disrespected you and your marriage. He wasn't even a good father to the boys. He was always yelling at them for no reason. I can't imagine why you would feel sorry for him."

"Mother, you know just because someone treats us wrong does not mean we should in return treat them wrong. You taught me that. Besides, she is so full of venom and anger, so bossy and demanding, she is going to make his life miserable. And I have lived in misery for a long time, I know how it feels."

"Amy, I didn't mean that you should treat him bad, just that feeling sorry for him is not fair after he treated you so poorly."

"Well, regardless of how he treated me, I have to do the right thing. I have to behave in a manner that I want my children to behave in. I have to think of them and set the example in the way I live and that I hope they will someday chose to live. Jesus told us we have to be forgiving of our fellow man and that includes ex-husbands. The boys are going to be home soon. Do you want to stay for dinner?"

"Do you think I should? I mean the boys will probably have lots of questions about today. I would hate to be in the way."

"Actually, I don't think they'll say much. We talked about everything. I have been honest with them, up to a point. There are some things I don't want them to know. I hope they never find out about the physical abuse and a few other things. They know about his girlfriend. They probably knew before I did."

"Sweetie, I hate to break it to you but the boys know about the abuse."

"How do you know? I never said anything to them about it and they've never said anything to me about it. Do you really think they know?"

"Yes, they know. They told me about it. I don't know why you think they don't know. They saw the bruises and heard all the fighting. They know you don't walk into doors and fall down or what ever it was that you told them happened. They're not that dumb."

"I suppose not. What else have they told you? I worry about how they feel, you know, deep inside. Do they hate their dad?"

"They've never said they hated him but they have said they were glad he was gone. I think they're relieved really. And I'm not sure I can blame them. I've noticed they seem more at peace. What are you going to cook for dinner? If you're making that awful casserole I know I'm not staying."

"What awful casserole? You mean that stuff with the beans and potatoes? I don't like it either, but Brandon loved it. I guess I never have to fix that again. Thank God. I thought about some burgers and fries. Something easy and then maybe a game of cards."

"Sounds good to me. I'll peel some potatoes for fries because I want real fries and not that frozen kind, if you don't mind. But I don't know about playing cards."

"The counselor at school told me to play games with Sean to build his math skills. We play games where he has to do addition and subtraction in his head. That way he doesn't realize he's learning. It's been good for him. His teacher said he's getting better and his attitude about school is improving. She said that would happen when he got more self-confident."

Screeching brakes a little while later indicated the bus had dropped the boys off. Sean stormed into the house, while Marshall ambled in. At fifteen, Marshall showed signs of maturity the other boys his age had not yet acquired. He was serious with his studies and showed little interest in the video games Sean relished. Sean was very much a seven year old child.

"Hey, Gram. What are you doing here?" Sean asked, as his grandmother met them at the door.

"What, can't a grandmother visit her favorite boys?"

"We're your only boys. Besides, wasn't today your garden club day?"

"Normally today would be my garden club day. But it was a bit too hot to get out and it was Mrs. Gorman's turn to host the club. She makes horrible tea and the worst cookies I have ever had. So I don't go when it's her turn."

"I thought at garden club you gardened," Sean said to his grandmother.

"It's not really a club where they garden all the time," Marshall interjected. "They talk about flowers and stuff while they drink tea and eat cookies. Besides, I know why you're really here. Today was court day for Mom and Dad. Is Mom okay?"

"Yes, she's fine. Everything's going to be okay. Just make sure you help her out as much as you can. Holding down a job, especially the one she has, and being both a mom and a dad to two growing young men is going to be hard."

Amy greeted the boys, trying to judge their feelings. "Hey, guys. How was school today? Marshall, did you finish that project you were working on?"

"Yeah. I think I did pretty good on it. The teacher said it was well done."

"I'm sure you did well, you worked so hard on it. Gram is going to stay for dinner. We're going to have some burgers and then maybe if everyone feels up to it, a game of cards. I haven't beaten anyone in a game lately."

As they sat down to eat, Amy watched Marshall pick at his burger. Sean ate with all the abandonment of a starved child. He seemed to be taking things in stride while his older brother was obviously brooding on something. She would have to remember to talk with him later. As they played their card game, Marshall seemed to rally a bit and join in more. He was still quiet and didn't laugh with the ease he had in the past. Amy hoped it was just another sign of his maturity and not due to the circumstances. Later that evening, after her mother had gone and the boys tucked in bed, Amy lay in her bed and thought about the events of the day. She had woke up that morning a married woman and gone to bed as a single woman. She could not help but to wonder what other changes each day would bring.

Suddenly, filled with fear and doubt about the future, she slid out of bed to her knees and began to cry. While part of her was relieved to be free of the abuse and the fear of her husband, another part was equally afraid she would not be strong enough to survive on her own and to take care of her sons like they deserved. How would she be able to work, take care of the household chores and take care of her children without any help? It would be an awesome task for anyone and she did not know if she was up to it. And yet she knew she had no choice but to forge ahead and do what was necessary for herself and her children.

Unable to form words to pray and sobbing uncontrollably, Amy could do little but let the tears flow. After a while, she began to feel a lessening of her grief. A verse from the Bible slipped into her head. How did it go?

"Peace I leave with you, my peace I give unto you: not as the world giveth, give I unto you. Let not your heart be troubled, neither let it be afraid." That was it. It was in John, she remembered. If there was anything she needed now, it was peace. As she sat on the floor beside her bed, her mind began to fill with the Bible lessons she had learned through the years. What was it, that Jesus was our high priest, that he had suffered as we suffer. Yes, abuse, abandonment and rejection he had known well. It was those things she was feeling now as well as the uncertainty of the future. But one thing she now realized, she was not having to go it alone. She began to feel at peace and knew that somehow everything was going to be alright. God was still in control.

Chapter Two

Amy made it through the rest of the week without incident. Saturday, she and the boys did some much needed yard work. She had tried to do all the mowing while the boys picked up sticks and whatever else was lying about in the yard. That proved to be more difficult than she had anticipated and she had to rely on Marshall to give her a break to catch her breath. Not used to the strenuous work that the yard required, she was worn out before lunch. Marshall had helped tremendously and she was very grateful.

She had to remember, as he had kept pointing out, that he was nearly grown and she didn't need to try to do everything herself. He was willing to help, all she had to do was ask. She was reluctant to ask, but she realized it had more to do with her not wanting to acknowledge his growing up than in trying to do everything on her own. Sean had to be reminded constantly that they were working in the yard and not playing. He frequently found a toy he had left in the yard and forgotten about. He stopped to play and she had to prod him to get back to work, which also brought out a bit of temper in him. There was not an ounce of quickening maturity on his part.

She had finished the front yard while the boys were cleaning up the back yard so it could be mowed next. She went to call them in for lunch and as she rounded the corner of the house she heard them talking.

"What do you think will happen to us?" Sean asked his brother.

"What do you mean, what will happen to us? Nothing is going to happen to us. Mom is going to take care of us," Marshall answered.

"You remember Kurt, that kid that lived down the street from Gram? His parents got divorced and he ended up living with the Fosters."

"Not with the Fosters, silly. In a foster home. That was because his parents were messed up. Remember they got in trouble with the police all the time. I heard that his dad beat him, you know, real bad. And his mother would go away and not take care of him. She would leave him home all alone without anybody to take care of him. That's not going to happen to us. Mom is a good mom and she will take good care of us. Don't worry about it," Marshall assured his brother.

"But what about Dad? Isn't he supposed to come get us sometimes to visit? He won't take good care of us. He don't even like us. Sometimes, a lot of times, he scares me. I'm afraid he'll beat us up like he used to do Mom."

"I don't think we really have to worry about that. I'm almost positive that we will never see him again. I'm glad that he and Mom got divorced. I hated it when he beat her up and yelled at us for no reason. He told me once that I was going to be a man just like him some day. But I don't want to be like him. I don't want my kids to feel about me the way I feel about my dad. I know he's our dad, but I'd rather he wasn't. I'd rather not have a dad than to have him for a dad," Marshall said.

"I know we're not supposed to hate him. That's what we learned in Sunday School, that hating people is wrong. But I don't like him much and I don't think I can pray for him

like the teacher said we were supposed to. We're supposed
to pray for people so they don't go to live with the devil. But
I think the devil is what makes him so mean."

"You know for a little kid, sometimes you can be real
smart. I think you're right about that. And I agree with you,
I don't know if I can pray for him either. Mom says we're
supposed to love him because he's our dad. But how can
you love someone who hits you for no reason and treats
everybody like dirt. I know he hit mom when he thought
we were in bed, but I listened at their door. That's not all he
did. He did things that wasn't right, that he would go to jail
for. I thought about calling the police once on him, but I was
afraid he'd think Mom did it and really beat her up. I glad
he's finally gone."

Amy realized that the boys had been hurt more than she
had thought, especially Marshall. She was sorry that they
had had to endure their father's intense anger and everything
he brought into the home. She wasn't sure Marshall knew
all that his father was into, but since he indicated it was
illegal he must know more than she thought he did. He must
of found out by listening at the door, at least she hoped that
was how. She'd hate to find out it was because he had found
some drugs in the house. She wasn't sure how Brandon
really felt about the boys. But she had a suspicion that
Marshall was right about his not coming back, and deep
down she hoped he was.

Not wanting them to know she had overheard their
conversation, she called out to them before she came around
the corner.

"Hey, guys. Are you up for some lunch? I'm tired and
need to take a break."

"Yeah, I'm hungry," said Sean. "Can we go to the
movies after lunch?"

"No, we can't. We've got to finish this yard today. And
you promised to clean your rooms, too. Besides you know

things have changed and we don't have as much money as when Dad was living here," Amy replied.

"You mean that we have to spend the whole day working, we don't get to have any fun? That's not fair!" Sean whined.

"Maybe once the yard is finished, instead of going to the movies, we can rent a movie and watch it at home. We can even pop some popcorn," Amy said, trying to soothe her son.

"Does that mean we don't have to clean our rooms today?" he asked gleefully.

"You wished," she told him, ruffling his hair. "When we finish the yard, which should be in a couple of hours, then we'll get cleaned up and go to the movie store. But you have to clean your rooms before we watch the movie so I can get your laundry done before bedtime. And you have to get your things ready for church tomorrow."

"Are we going to our regular church?" asked Marshall, as he slathered mustard on a piece of bread, making his typical ham, cheese and potato chip sandwich.

"Of course, why wouldn't we," Amy asked.

"I just thought, um, well, we'll be the only family in church that's divorced," he answered.

"No we won't. Lydia is divorced. And so is Mrs. Collier."

"I didn't know Mrs. Collier was divorced. She's kind of old so I thought her husband was dead. And Lydia doesn't come anymore. At least I haven't seen her daughter lately. Sean, what's her daughter's name? She was in your Sunday School class and you used to play with her at school."

"Her name is Carlie," he said with a mouth full of chips.

"Don't talk with your mouth full, your spraying chips everywhere," Amy scolded her son.

"I was just answering a question. If you don't want me to talk with food in my mouth, don't ask me questions when I'm eating."

Amy rolled her eyes at his remark. "Hurry and finish your lunch so we can get back to work. The quicker we finish the yard the sooner we get out of here to get a movie."

After lunch, she and the boys went out to tackle the rest of the yard. As predicted, the job was finished in a couple of hours and she sent them in to bathe while she put the yard tools and lawnmower away. Looking over the yard, she was satisfied with what she saw. Feeling a sense of accomplishment, she went in looking forward to her own bath.

Cleaned and refreshed, Amy went to check on the boys. Marshall was in his room listening to music. Sean was in the living room playing a video game.

"Are you guys ready to go?" she called.

"Sure Mom. Let me save my game," Sean answered.

Marshall turned his stereo off and headed for the door. Sean followed a few moments later. As they gathered in the hall at the door, Amy looked at Sean. His hair was still sweat slicked and he had dirt rings around his neck.

"Did you take a bath?" she asked him.

"Was I supposed to take one? I put on clean clothes," he replied, somewhat indignant.

"Son! You were sweaty and dirty. Why would you put clean clothes on a dirty body? You know better than that. I think you were too eager to get in there and play that game. When we get home you are going to take a bath and then clean your room. No more games today and none tomorrow."

"Mom, that's not fair! Am I going to get to watch the movie?"

"Yes, you can watch the movie, providing you get through with your room in time. Come on let's go."

Later that evening as Amy and Marshall watched the movie, eating freshly popped popcorn, she felt a twinge of guilt. Sean had not obeyed her. After his bath, he had went in his room and shut the door and played with his toys instead of cleaning his room as he had been told to do. Amy had to punish him by not allowing him to watch the movie. He was angry and had slammed his door, whining that everybody was mean to him. She seemed to always be punishing him lately. But he refused to do as he was told and responded with temper tantrums. He had been spending a lot of time in his room, denied permission to play his video games. Still, he continued to act out and misbehave. He had a stubbornness that exhausted her.

Although feeling guilty that he could not enjoy watching the movie he had helped pick out, Amy knew she had to punish him yet again. She didn't want him to think she did not love him or loved him less than Marshall. Marshall hardly ever got in trouble, she thought. How odd that two children from the same environment to be so vastly different. And while Sean was being punished, she couldn't enjoy his company and that too grieved her.

That evening as she tucked Sean in bed, she tried to explain to him about obedience. It was important for him to learn to obey those in authority. She told him that he had to learn to obey because it would be something he would have to do through every aspect of is life. He would have to not only obey his mother but teachers, police officers, the laws of the land and someday a boss. He had to obey not just because she said he did, but because God expected him to and had in fact commanded him to. She had talked to him about this before but sometimes he just did not do as he was told. He said it was not fun or not fair and sometimes he just forgot what he was told to do. He was more stubborn when it came to doing things he didn't enjoy, like cleaning his room. She explained that life was not always fun or fair, but that didn't mean certain things didn't have to be done. She told him she understood that he just wanted to have fun but he had to learn to help out and be more agreeable. She told him she loved him and missed the times they spent together playing cards or other games or just talking. But until he learned to mind and do as he was told, without the tantrums, he would have to be punished. After her loving lecture, she went off to her own room. She again pondered the difference in the boys as she lay in her bed.

The next morning she went in to wake them for church. Returning to her own room, she thought about the remark Marshall made about them being the only divorced family in the church. The same thought had occurred to her previously. Amy wondered why Lydia had quit coming to church, if it was because she too was recently divorced. Lydia and her husband had both gone to church and Amy was surprised when she had heard about them splitting up. She was even more surprised when she learned about Carl's affair. As soon as the news was out about Lydia and Carl, Lydia stopped coming to church. Amy would have to call her and see how she was doing.

As they drove to church, Marshall talked non stop about everything that came into his head. As of late he had been quiet, lost in his own thoughts, so Amy could tell he was nervous but not entirely sure why. They had gone to church every Sunday, even after Brandon had moved out. Everybody knew some of the ugly details about what had occurred in her marriage. She fought against hiding in shame over her disastrous marriage, feeling that she would be judged poorly because of her husband's behavior and their ultimate split and divorce. She had been embarrassed about it but was afraid if she quit going to church it would be harder to go back later. And she feared that it would show she had some guilt to hide. She chose to continue attending church as if nothing had happened and indulge in her faith.

She needed to be in the house of God with other Christians. Besides, it was her faith that had gotten her this far. She had known others that seemed to go off the deep end, doing some pretty stupid things, after going through a divorce. She felt her Christian beliefs had kept her grounded and had kept her from falling apart. She hadn't been tempted to "drown her sorrows" knowing it would end no where good.

As they got to church, Sean ran off to join his class. Marshall just stood beside the car.

"Marshall, it won't be as bad as you imagine it will. No one will think poorly of you just because your parents are divorced. They didn't think poorly of you when we were separated, did they? Don't worry about it. Your friends all like you, nothing will change. Come on, I'll walk in with you."

Amy put on a brave face, but inside she wondered if he had a reason to be concerned. She could not let him know she felt the same fear. She remembered a preacher she had heard when she was a child. He had said that real Christians did not get divorced. They had made a covenant before God and only by death was it broken. But Brandon had broken his covenant, not her. And if she understood the Bible, adultery was an acceptable reason for divorce. Besides, she didn't think she would ever marry again anyway.

Entering the building, they were greeted as they always were. Craig, Marshall's best friend, called out to him. Amy felt him relax when he saw his friend. She wished she had such a friend. She had not gotten close to anyone because of her marriage problems. Now she wished she had.

Chapter Three

Amy felt refreshed as she always did after church. Somehow, going to church made her feel as if she had bathed the filth of the world off, feeling clean inside and out. It was a feeling she relished. The worship service was uplifting and the message was enlightening. She was glad she had not given in to the temptation to stay home.

Marshall asked if he could go home with Craig and then come back to church that evening with him. Amy felt it would be good for him and told him to have fun. Sean asked if he too could spend the afternoon with one of his friends. She reminded him that he was grounded and could not play any video games. She knew he would do just that with any friend he went home with so she told him he had to come home with her. Sean began to whine that it was not fair, that Marshall got to do anything he wanted. Amy told him that was not true. Marshall had less of a tendency to misbehave so he got to enjoy more freedoms, something Sean needed to learn. She told him that although he could not play any games, he could watch the movie he had missed the night before. While he would have preferred to play his games, he liked watching movies almost as much.

After lunch, while Sean was occupied with his movie, Amy thought about calling Lydia. She hesitated because she wasn't sure what to say. She didn't want her to think the only reason she called was because they shared being divorced. She was concerned about why she had quit coming to church. Dialing her number, Amy had to force herself not to hang the phone up. Part of her hoped that Lydia wasn't home and the call could be made at a later time. But she had to admit that even later would be difficult.

"Hello," a young voice answered.

"Carlie?" Amy asked.

"Yes," was the timid answer.

"Is your mother home?" What a dumb question, of course she would be home if her daughter was home, Amy thought.

"Mommy, it's for you. It's some lady," Amy heard Carlie tell her mother.

"Hello," Lydia answered.

"Hi, Lydia, this is Amy. I haven't seen you and Carlie in a while. How are you doing?"

"Oh, Amy, hi. We're doing okay. How are you? I heard about your divorce. Is everything okay? I know how hard divorce is."

"I guess I'm okay. There are times when I feel like the world is spinning out of control. I get afraid that I won't be able to do everything that needs to be done, or take care of the boys like they deserve. How did you hear about it?"

"I ran into your ex a couple of weeks ago. He was with some crazy woman. You know how I am, I asked him what he was doing with another woman. She told me that he had left you and was getting a divorce. I guess he couldn't speak for himself. I told her I wasn't talking to her so she could just keep her mouth shut. She pushed him away and he never said anything. I suppose she rules the roost, huh. So, how's the boys taking all this?"

Amy laughed at her friend's boldness. She didn't know how much Lydia knew about the cause of the divorce and what had taken place. She figured she probably knew more than most though. She and Brandon had frequented the restaurant Lydia managed and he had boldly taken his girlfriend there. It was Lydia that first made her aware of Brandon's latest infidelity. It was especially embarrassing since she and Lydia attended church together though they were not real close as friends. Amy had suspected Brandon had begun another affair but it was hard to accept in reality. Somehow it made her feel that she was not much of a wife or a woman if she could not keep her husband at home.

"The boys are taking it pretty well," Amy replied. "In fact I over heard them talking about it and they seem relieved. You know, I thought I hid everything from them. I'm sure there are things they don't know, and don't need to know, but there is a lot they do know. And I'm doing okay, I guess. But for some reason I feel like I did something wrong. I feel ashamed, like I should be wearing a scarlet letter or something. Why is that? Did you ever feel that way?"

"Yeah, I did. I've talked to other women that felt the same way. There is this belief that anytime a marriage goes wrong, it's the woman's fault. My mother even told me that if I had been a better wife, Carl wouldn't have left me for another woman. I thought I did everything I could to keep him from leaving after his affair began. I told him I would forgive him but he was set on leaving. I thought he didn't want a wife. He wanted a wife, just not me as that wife. He told me that he had fallen in love with someone else and wanted to be with her. He loves Carlie and is a good father. His new wife is a nice woman and they do seem to be in love. It makes me angry that he is so happy with his new life and it makes me angry that I'm bothered by it. I want to be as happy as he is. But things could be worse.

"I have a woman who works for me and she has gone through a really ugly divorce. Her husband cheated on her with any willing thing that came along, flaunted it in her face. She was pregnant with her third child when she decided she had had enough. He told her their marriage would be fine if she would just accept his lifestyle. He said men were made to have a variety of women. She was really torn. She was afraid of what kind of life she would be able to offer the children without a father, just as you are. But she felt it was in her best interest to move on without him. After her baby was born she came to work for me and she has been a wonderful worker. I have seen her grow stronger and more secure. Amy, you're a strong woman, you'll be just fine. Brandon will have to deal with whatever his problems are one day," Lydia said.

"Well, I don't know what Brandon's problems are. I thought everything was okay, not great but okay. I suppose there were signs that I missed. Then suddenly it was like he just went crazy. He came home from work angry one day and just kept getting angrier. We were eating supper one evening and he flew into a rage and knocked the dishes off the table. I sent Marshall and Sean to their rooms, just to keep them out of his way. When I walked into our bedroom, he hit me so hard it knocked me out.

"He apologized but never explained what it was all about. After that, I never knew what would set him off. I lived in fear and worried what would happen to the boys if he turned on them. Then I found out about a woman he had been with and that he had started doing drugs. He said the drugs helped him deal with the stress of his job. I knew I should get away from him, but I didn't know how to do it. He and I got married right out of school and I had never really been on my own. And I had always believed in until death do you part.

"You hear about women who put up with cheating, abusive men and wonder why they put up with it. Well, I know why. They think they have no other options. I really prayed for God to help me. Perhaps this woman he got involved with is really a blessing. Now I'm free from that abuse and the boys are safe. I don't know if he would have hurt them but that was always my fear," Amy said.

"Hey, how about us getting together sometimes? I bet we could swap some stories. I'd invite you over but my apartment is so small it's hard to turn around in. But maybe we can take the kids to the park sometime. I have to tell you, I've missed having someone to talk to."

"That sounds great. You are Carlie are welcomed to come to our house. We could rent the kids some movies and you and I could talk. You could even stay the night. We have plenty of room and would enjoy the company."

"Sounds like fun. Thanks. Carlie is going to be in the play at school. She said Sean got a part, too. What's he going to be? Carlie is a butterfly and she is so excited."

"Sean is a frog. He hopped around croaking all day when he found out. My mother is making his costume. She is a wonder with needle and thread. I can't even sew a button on."

"I'm having some problems with Carlie's costume. Do you think your mom can help me out? Sewing isn't really my cup of tea either."

"Oh, I'm sure she would. She is one of those people that can make a silk purse from a sow's ear."

"What? How do you make a silk purse from a pig's ear? And who would want to and why would you want one?" Lydia asked, laughing.

"I don't know. That's an expression my grandmother used to use. I never understood it but it describes my mother very well. She can sew anything. I'll talk to her for you."

"Thanks. I appreciate that."

"Well, I hate to cut this conversation short but I have got to get Sean up and ready for church. Would you be interested in joining us? I'd love the company."

"I haven't been to church in a while. I was a little uncomfortable the last time I went. I think I'll pass right now but I'll give it some thought. Thanks for asking. I'll talk to you later."

Amy was so glad she had called. Perhaps she could encourage Lydia to come back to church. It would be good for both her and Carlie. She needed to make a note to talk to her mother about Carlie's costume or she would forget. The play was two weeks away, maybe she should plan a get together with Lydia and Carlie after the play.

"Sean, you need to turn the TV off and get ready for church," she called to her son.

Not hearing a response, she went to check on him. He was fast asleep with the TV blaring. How could he sleep with all that noise, she wondered? Waking him, she told him get ready for church and not to forget to wash his face and brush his teeth. He groggily did as he was told.

On the way to church she asked him why he didn't tell her Carlie was in his play. He said he forgot and asked her how she knew. When she told him about talking to Carlie's mom and was thinking about inviting them over after the play he looked at her funny.

"What is that look for?" she asked.

"You're not trying to make her my girlfriend, are you?" he questioned.

"No, but I hadn't thought of that. She's really cute, don't you think?" his mother teased.

"Mom! I'm only seven, I'm too young to have a girlfriend. I'm not even sure I like girls. Carlie is okay, I mean she's cool for a girl but I don't want a girlfriend."

"Okay. That's fine, you can wait another year or two," she laughed.

"If Carlie doesn't have to be my girlfriend, it would be fun for her and her mom to come over after the play. It would be like a party, huh? Can Stevie come over, too?"

23

"We'll see. I don't want you running around at church. If you're going to sit with your friends, you are going to have to sit still and quiet. No playing, do you hear me?"

"Yes ma'am. I'm going to sit with Mickey and he has to sit with his mom and dad. We'll be quiet or she'll pinch us. And she pinches hard."

"And I'll be watching you. Just remember that."

Sean ran off to find Mickey while Amy went to find her usual seat. Sitting in her spot, was a man she had never seen before. At first she felt a little perturbed, then she realized that it was silly. It wasn't as if the pew belonged to her. She decided to go and welcome him to the church.

"Hi. My name is Amy Alexander. I don't think I have seen you visit us before. Is this the first time you've been here before?"

"Hello. Yes, this is my first time here. My name is Greg Jansen."

"It's nice to meet you. Are you new around here?"

"Yeah, I just moved into town. I pass the church on my way to work and thought I'd try it out."

"That's great. Please come back again. We're glad to have you."

Amy was glad to see some new faces in the church. After the service she'd have to remember to introduce Mr. Jansen around to some of the other members. She wondered if he was married and had any children. She would really like for the children's ministries to grow. The teachers were doing a great job with all the kids. She had seen some difference in her kids since they had been attending Sunday School regularly.

Amy thought that perhaps she should get more involved with the church. She had been attending long enough she should be doing something besides being a spectator. She would have to talk to the pastor to see if there was something she could do in the church. And she'd pray about it. God would lead her in the right direction.

Chapter Four

Amy joined Lydia at the school play and together they shared an evening of laugher. The second grade class put on a wonderful play. Even though lines were forgotten and mistakes were made, the children and their parents enjoyed the production. Carlie didn't want to take her butterfly costume off after the play. Because Lydia and Carlie were coming to their house after the play, Sean chose to keep his costume on also. Having finally given in to Sean's repeated pleadings about Stevie also coming over after the play, he and his mother and sister would join them.

Amy had met Stevie during lunches at the school with Sean. She had never met his mother and was a little nervous at the prospect. She had taken some pains to prepare treats for the kids, making cookies in the shapes of the things they had portrayed in the play and punch she called "pond water." It seemed that Sean was as excited about the party as he was about the play. Sean, with Stevie in tow, ran up to his mother.

"We're ready to go," he shouted excitedly.

"We can't go without Stevie's mother," Amy told her son. Turning to his friend she said, "Hello, Stevie. Where is your mom?"

"She's coming. My sister had to go to the bathroom. She's waiting on her."

Amy had almost forgotten about Stevie's sister. Sean had not known anything about her except that she was older than Stevie. Why would his mother need to take an older child to the bathroom? That was certainly odd.

"My sister didn't want to come to the party. She said she didn't want to hang out all night with old ladies and little kids. But Mom told her she had to, so she's kind of mad. There they are," Stevie said.

Looking up, Amy saw a woman nearly dragging a teenage girl. It was undoubtedly Stevie's mother and sister. The girl looked as if she was going to attend a funeral, dressed completely in black clothing. It was on obvious statement of her feelings. With her attire and her angry expression, she looked like more than a handful for her mother. She hoped there would be no problems that would ruin the evening for the kids.

"Hello, I'm Karen and this is my daughter Lacy. You must be Sean's mom. It's good to meet you. Stevie talks about Sean all the time. Thank you for inviting us over this evening."

"Hello, it's good to meet both of you," she said. "This is Lydia and her daughter Carlie. They're joining us this evening."

Lacy mumbled, "Great, more old ladies and little kids."

Karen looked embarrassed at her daughter's remark. Amy acted like she had not heard it and lead the way to the parking lot.

"I don't live too far from here, if you want to follow me to the house. Sean tied balloons to the mailbox so you wouldn't miss the house," she said.

On the short drive home, Sean asked his mother if Lacy was going to ruin his party. Amy certainly hoped not and was a little angry that the girl had been dragged along against her will. She looked old enough to have been able to stay home alone for a short time.

"Why do you think Stevie's mom made her come if she didn't want to," Amy asked her son.

"Stevie said his mother and sister fight all the time. She gets in trouble a lot at home. I don't think his mother trusts her to stay at home when she's gone. Even I know to stay at home when you tell me to."

"You mean like that time I went next door to use the neighbor's phone to call the phone company when ours was broke? I told you to ride your bike in the driveway and not to leave the yard and you rode down the street to Gram's house."

"That's when I learned to stay at home. I was grounded from my bike for a month."

"Not a month, two weeks. It should not have taken being punished to learn to obey what you're told to do but I'm glad you learned."

Pulling into the driveway, Amy saw both cars behind her. She lead the group into the house.

"This is my mother, Sarah Randolph, and my oldest son, Marshall. Mom, this is Karen, Lacy, and Stevie. My mother was at the play but she came home ahead of us to get everything ready. Thanks Mom."

"Hello, it's good to meet all of you. Carlie, you make a beautiful butterfly. Sean and Stevie, I haven't seen a finer frog or dragonfly than you two. Come on it and sit down. Would any of you like anything to drink? Kids, we have some pond water, complete with fish and turtle eggs. Would you like some?"

Sarah led the kids into the kitchen for cookies and drinks. They wanted to see the turtle eggs. Sarah had put white grapes and gummy fish in the punch. Marshall had commented that the fish looked dead floating in the punch, which got him a punch of his own from his grandmother. Amy took the others into the living room and tried to think of something to say. She was not very good at entertaining and was afraid her nervousness would show.

"Lacy, what grade are you in?" asked Lydia.

"Why?" asked Lacy.

"I was just wondering. I have a niece in the eighth grade and was wondering if you might know her."

"I'm in high school, not junior high. I'm in the eleventh grade, if you must know."

"Oh, that would make you smart enough to know that being rude won't make you any friends."

Lacy gave Lydia an angry look and then stalked out of the room to find the younger kids.

"I'm sorry about Lacy. I would have preferred to leave her at the house, which is what she wanted. But she has a tendency to disappear. I think she sneaks out to be with a boyfriend but she says she doesn't have one. I don't know where she goes or who she's with. She says she goes away to be by herself. I'm kind of at a loss about what to do with her sometimes," Karen said.

"Not to be rude, but where is her dad? Sometimes girls do better for their dads than their moms. I know I did. My dad had more influence over me than my mom. Even today I'm closer to him than her. I guess I will always be a daddy's girl," Lydia said.

"He's around. She sees him when she wants. Right now she's mad that he remarried. His wife is a nice woman but Lacy is still angry. Stevie likes her a lot and I guess that's good. I hope Lacy comes around. She'll miss a lot by cutting him out of her life."

"You speak well of your ex-husband. Do you and he get along?" asked Amy, entering the conversation.

"Yes, we parted on good terms. We married young and then realized that we had nothing in common, nothing to hold a marriage together. We weren't really in love at the time, we were just too young to know it. We tried to make it work, especially when the kids came along. But it just didn't work. Stevie was young and really doesn't remember our being together. Lacy does and thinks I should have done more to keep him home. She doesn't care if anyone is happy but her. I just hope we didn't hurt the kids too badly by separating, that they'll be okay. Am I correct to assume that your and your husband are divorced?"

"Yes. It's only been about a month. Lydia is divorced too. How long has it been since you got divorced, Lydia?"

"Almost a year now. Carlie sees her dad on his weekends and seems to be fine with that. He's remarried and has always been a great dad. I'm getting settled into being single. It was hard at first but I'm getting used to it now. And Carlie is a great companion. She's my support sometimes."

"Yeah, I wouldn't know what to do without the kids," said Amy.

"Well, I have been divorced for over six years. And I haven't settled into anything. I dated a guy for a while but he had a real problem with the kids. Amazingly, Lacy liked him. He was a veterinarian and she loves animals. She tried to talk to him but he wasn't interested. Stevie didn't like him at all. He's had me all to himself since he was born, except for Lacy, and he doesn't want to share. I hate the dating scene. Some women really enjoy it, but I just want to meet a man and settle down."

Amy saw her mother peek around the corner and give her a thumbs up. She supposed that was to mean she felt everything was going okay. She could hear the kids laughing in the other room so perhaps it was.

"Karen, would you be interested in coming to church with us on Sunday? Amy and I go to the same church. It would be great if you could join us. And it might be good for Lacy as well," Lydia said.

Amy looked at her friend. Lydia looked back at her and nodded her head. She was excited that Lydia had invited Karen to join them at church, which meant that Lydia was planning to come back. But she was ashamed that she had not thought to invite Karen herself.

"I don't know. I've tried to do the right things all my life and raise my kids right. I don't think I'm bad. Not to say I don't make mistakes, but I think I'm okay. I don't think I need to get saved, what ever that means. I've just never been big on church," Karen said.

Karen's comment struck a cord in Amy.

"People misunderstand the saved concept. They think of it like being saved from drowning and they don't see themselves as drowning. That's the problem with that concept. To understand salvation, you have to understand what sin is. Sin is not just killing and robbing and lying. Sin is not living for God, but for ourselves. It is anything that prevents us from being in a right relationship with God. Being good and doing the right thing is not the same thing as living for God. Salvation is about being redeemed, it's about hope, it's about being in a personal relationship with our heavenly father.

"Being redeemed is trading a life of sin for a life free from sin. When Christ died on the cross, his blood washed sin from us. We became clean. The Bible says we were bound to death because of that sin and he redeemed us through his own death. We can have eternal life, not life here on earth as we know it, but life eternally with him. That's where I think the term saved comes from. He has saved us for himself. And who would not want that. I'm sorry for going on like that. I just feel passionate about my faith," Amy said.

"Mom, I want to go," Lacy said, interrupting the conversation.

The women turned to look at Lacy, not having heard her come into the room.

"Sweetheart, I'm not ready to go just yet. We'll leave in a little bit," Karen said.

"I would like to go home. Now," Lacy insisted.

"Not now, I said. Go play with the other kids."

"I'm not a kid," Lacy said through clenched teeth. She stormed off into the other room.

"I don't know. We'll see," Karen said, turning back to the women.

Later that evening after Karen and her children left, Amy and Lydia rearranged the living room. Lydia and Carlie were going to stay the night and Sean had decided he and Carlie were going camp out for the night. Only they were camping in the living room and sheets were being erected as a tent. After getting their teeth brushed, the kids crawled into their tent and began making up scary tales. The tales usually ended up in laughter instead of terror. Amy and Lydia sat on Amy's bed and talked.

"You know it's not so much that I'm not married, it's more that I hate not having a partner. Every where you go, there's couples holding hands or looking into each other's eyes. I feel like a freak and just want to go hide," Lydia said.

"Yeah, I know what you mean. I went to lunch the other day and there was a couple there that was practically making out. I was embarrassed just witnessing it. Then when I got to my car, I realized I missed having someone to hold my hand or kiss me. Which was kind of bizarre because Brandon and I hadn't done that in a long time. But I guess I missed it before that and only then realized what I had been missing," Amy said.

"They've always said that you don't know what you've got until you've lost it. I guess it's truer than I realized. Another problem I have is going out by myself. Carlie went to her dad's one weekend and I decided to go see a movie. I drove to the theater and parked. Got out of the car and got in line. As I was standing there with all the other people, I realized that I was the only one there by myself. I just left. I couldn't go to the movies alone. I felt like I was the only single person on the face of the earth. I imagined everybody looking at me and feeling sorry for me because I didn't have a partner."

"I haven't experienced that yet. I hadn't even thought of that but I think I would feel the same way. Even when I was still married, I couldn't make myself go places by myself. I went places I could take the boys, they were always my companions. Sometimes I just wanted another adult to talk to. I guess it'll be worse now. Marshall is growing up and I seem to be doing more without him. Sean has limited interests so our choices are few. What do you do, just not go anywhere?"

"Pretty much. I went to dinner with some friends but they drank a lot and wanted to go to a bar afterwards. I refused to go to the bar and they never invited me to go with them again. There's not a lot of things for single people to do that doesn't involve drinking and picking up someone of the opposite sex."

"You and I could do some things. We could see a girly movie and have dinner or go shopping can't we?"

"Of course. And I expect us to. I finally have someone like me to do things with. No more eating delivery pizza in the living room with a rented movie by myself. But what do you think about dating?"

"I don't."

"You don't what?"

"I don't think about dating. I mean where would you meet someone you could trust, someone that's not just out for fun? Brandon's really the only person I've ever dated. I don't even know how to anymore."

"Do you think it's changed?"

"I think so. I mean with the women's lib movement, women ask men out and things like that. I don't know the rules anymore. Who pays, who decides where you go or what you do, what do you wear? I just don't know what goes anymore. It's foreign territory to me."

"I never thought about that. But I would like to go out on a date, to feel that tingle of excitement again."

"Excitement? Is that what you called it. I thought it was fear. I was always afraid of rejection. I guess that was why I stuck with dating Brandon. He seemed to accept me so I hung with him."

"Why did you stay with him for so long? Didn't he hit you? I mean I saw some bruises a couple of times."

"He did hit me. I'm not really sure why I stayed. I think it was because I felt I had no other choice. He was my husband, I had made a commitment in marrying him. He was the father of my children and I wanted my children to grow up in a two parent home. I tried to make the best of things, to not just give up when it got hard. I felt like I was the problem and I got what I deserved."

"That's nonsense. You did not deserve to get hit because he had a bad day at the office or because his girlfriend was unavailable or what ever excuse he gave you. You put up with a lot but I understand what you're saying. Carl was good to me and I guess I'm lucky in that respect. Our breakup was my fault but I can't cry about it now. But I still think I might like to try dating."

"You're a brave soul," Amy said as she snuggled down in bed. "I'll leave the dating to you."

Lydia laughed. The two were asleep a short while later.

Chapter Five

Amy was paying bills, trying to see if she had enough in her budget to treat the boys to a special day in town. She wanted to take a whole day and take them to the museum and science center and then to a nice dinner. She wanted them to enjoy an evening of "fine" dining, something she thought they would look forward to. She knew they would enjoy the museum and science center because they had been there before but the restaurant she had picked out for dinner was more upscale than they were accustomed to. Amy had a second motive for the dinner scheme as well. Marshall was becoming a young man and dating was not to far off his horizon. She wanted him to know how to conduct himself in such situations. This was one of those times a dad would have come in handy. She had tried to talk to him about the "birds and bees" but it embarrassed him badly. He said he knew all he needed to know. She wasn't so sure about that but then again kids today knew a lot more than their parents did at the same age.

As she was working on her budget, she was interrupted by Sean. He apparently had some things on his mind.

"Stevie went to visit his dad this weekend. He doesn't like going to his dad's sometimes unless Lacy goes and she doesn't want to go because their dad has a new wife. Stevie likes her but Lacy doesn't. His dad has a baby and he wants Stevie and Lacy to come visit to see the baby so he'll know who they are. Stevie said his mom told him his dad is a good guy. If he was a good guy why did he divorce Stevie's mom? I thought only bad dads divorced the moms," Sean questioned his mother.

"No, not just bad dads divorce the moms. Sometimes parents just don't get along and they think that it would be best if they separated. It's not because either the mom or the dad is bad. Stevie's parents are friends, they just didn't want to be married anymore," Amy tried to explain.

"I don't understand. Why do people get married if they don't want to be married? I don't think I will ever get married. It's too confusing," Sean commented.

"I know it's confusing. Karen said she and Stevie's dad married when they were still pretty young. A lot of people do that and then find out after they get a little older that they were not really in love. They still want to find someone that they can love and have a good life with. I guess that's what happened with Karen and her husband."

"Why don't they wait until they are old enough to know if they really love each other instead of getting married before they know?"

"Well, sometimes, most times really, they think they are old enough and know what they're doing. It's like ordering a large pizza because you're hungry and then after eating part of it you realize you weren't as hungry as you thought. Or thinking you want to buy a video game and after you spent your money on it you find you don't really like it. You realize you didn't want it until it was too late. Make sense?"

"I guess so. Is that what happened with you and Dad? You found out too late you didn't love each other?"

"Well, yes and no. To tell you the truth, I don't know what happened with me and your dad. I thought we loved each other. I know I loved him but I guess he didn't really love me. But I don't really know because he never said."

Sean appeared to reflect on their conversation. Amy knew it was a lot for a little boy to get a grasp on. She hoped that even though her marriage ended disastrously, he would have an opportunity to have a loving relationship of his own one day. She didn't want him to be discouraged before he even began to seek such a relationship.

After a while, Amy prepared a simple lunch for the two of them. Marshall was off with a friend working on a school assignment. Before she was through with lunch, her mother showed up at her door.

"I wasn't expecting you for lunch. If you had let me know you were coming I would've prepared something more than tuna sandwiches," Amy told her mother as she let her into the house.

"Well, I didn't plan on coming for lunch. But I have been putting off this chore for a few weeks and if I don't take care of it soon it's going to snowball on me," Sarah told her daughter.

"What chore?"

"Go on and finish your lunch and then we'll talk about it. Sean, how is school? You used to let me know what grades you were making and what you were learning in school. Are you getting too old to tell me about school?"

"I'm doing okay. Second grade is harder than first grade. I don't think I like second grade. I'm finished eating. Can I go play now?" he asked, getting up from the table.

"I suppose so," Amy told him. She would have to remember to call the school this week. Her mother was right, he was usually more verbal about school. Amy wondered if there was something wrong.

"So, mother. What is it we need to talk about?" she asked as soon as Sean was out of the room. Her mother looked more nervous than she'd ever seen her look. She was immediately concerned. "You're not going to tell me you're about to get married, are you?" she teased, trying to keep her worry at bay.

"Um, yes. That is what I'm going to tell you. Loren and I are planning to get married around Christmas. That way everyone will be able to come to the celebration. Kevin and his family should be able to come as well as Loren's children and their families."

37

"Mom, that's only two months away. What if everybody already has Christmas plans. You know Kevin, he makes plans a year in advance. Have you even met this man's kids? And by the way, since you have already decided to marry this person, why have I not met him? I knew you were going to dinner with a man from your book club, but marriage? Are you sure?"

"Amy. I am sure, very sure. Loren Kessler is the man I have always dreamed of being with. After your father left, I was so relieved. I never wanted to get married again but when I met Loren, I began to think about what it would be like to be loved, to be cherished. I never had that and I want it. And Loren gives me that. Think about it Amy. Do you know what it is like to be cherished? Don't you want that?"

"I don't know, I suppose. But the idea of putting my life back in a man's control scares me. I don't think I can do that."

"Married is not about control. Marriage is about love and honor, about sharing and companionship. You've not experienced that yet. Brandon didn't love you, not really. And he didn't honor your marriage. Your whole marriage was about him. I wished I could've stopped you from marrying him. Don't let your marriage to Brandon keep you from finding someone that will truly love you and treat you like you deserve."

"Mom, what was your marriage like to Dad? I mean, I never saw any affection between you. What kept you together those years when Kevin and I was growing up and then for him to leave once I was out of the house?"

"There was nothing between us. We got married because that's what everybody thought we should do. We only dated a few weeks and didn't really know each other. I didn't know at the time he loved someone else. His father didn't like the girl so he pushed us to get married. My parents thought it was good because they wouldn't have to support me anymore. We tried to make the best of it, especially after you kids came along. But you were just a few months old when he told me he didn't love me and never would.

"Curtis said we would stay together and he would take care of me and the babies but he would always love the girl he was with before we were married. He decided that once you were gone he didn't need to stay anymore. He had been seeing the woman the whole time we had been married. She had never married and they had three children of their own. He spent enough time here for people to think we had a decent marriage but the rest of the time he spent with his other family. I knew about what was going on but it seemed best to let it alone. He married her as soon as our divorce was final. I met her and the other children when he was in the hospital. We talked a little. She really loved him. I felt sorry for her. They had only been married for a short while before he died."

Amy was amazed by her mother's story. She had no idea what had transpired during her parent's marriage. She knew her father was gone a lot but she thought it was because of his business. And to learn that she had three half siblings was a shock.

"I never thought Dad loved Kevin or me. I guess that wasn't just my imagination. You met his other kids? How did that make you feel?"

"I was hurt. Not for myself but for you and Kevin. Although he was distant with you and Kevin, he was apparently a good father to the other kids. The oldest is named after him. He seemed to understand what was going on, with his dad married to one woman but having a family with another one. You and Kevin were not really recognized as his children. You were referred to as my children. Curtis' mother must have known about it as well. I haven't seen

39

her since the funeral but she knew Curtis' other family and seemed close to the woman and her children."

"Really? I'm her legitimate grandchild and I didn't even know her."

"Well, don't lose any sleep over that. It has nothing to do with you. So, you're not angry about me getting married again? I'm going to need you to help me make plans. I want you to stand up as my maid of honor. I'm hoping that Kevin will be agreeable and will give me away. You don't think that's corny do you? I know he's coming down for Christmas. "

"I'm surprised but not angry. I just want you to be happy. And who knows what Kevin will think. But if he has a problem with it, Marshall will be honored to give you away."

"I had figured for him to be my backup. I'm planning dinner at my house next Saturday. Loren will be there, and hopefully his son and his family, so you can get acquainted with the your soon-to-be step-brother."

"Sounds good. Mom? Did you have problems adjusting to life as a divorcee?"

"What do you mean? Like feeling as if people were looking at me because I didn't have a husband? Or feeling like an oddball at gatherings were there were two parents raising a child instead of just one? My difficulties began long before your father and I divorced. He was never around even when we were married. I felt like a single parent before I actually became one. I had a woman ask me once if I had ever been married. She thought since I never attended any functions with a husband that I wasn't married even though I had two children. It was very embarrassing."

"Really? I guess I hadn't thought about that. I mean my marriage to Brandon wasn't much different than yours to Dad. And even though I'm divorced with my children still young, you were really a single parent too, just not divorced."

"That's right. And I faced many of the same situations divorced parents do. Only Curtis continued to support us instead of abandoning his responsibility. I guess I can say that about him. He wasn't a bad man, he just didn't love us."

"If you had it all to do over again, would you?"

"I would. Even with his absence in the house, the lack of companionship, the lack of a loving relationship, I got you and Kevin out of our marriage and I wouldn't have wanted to miss that for anything. You were great kids and you filled a great void in my life. I know that I wasn't there for you like I should have but it didn't mean I didn't love you. Look, I've got to run. We'll finish this conversation later."

Sarah kissed Amy on the forehead and headed out the door. Amy thought about her mother's life and how it was similar to her own. She realized that her mother's experience gave her some insight into what Amy was going through. She felt a stronger connection to her mother and a greater sense of respect. She wished though that she had found that connection earlier in her life and not missed opportunities to develop a closer relationship with her mother. But she was glad that she had it now.

Chapter Six

The next couple of weeks were hectic for Amy. With working and helping to make wedding plans for her mother, Amy had forgotten to call the school and check on Sean. While sorting through work orders, an unexpected call sent Amy's regular chaos to new a new level. Snatching up the ringing phone, Amy anticipated another customer with a problem.

"Hello, how can I help you today?" she asked.

"Mrs. Alexander, this is Clair Todd, Sean's principal. We need for you and your husband to attend a meeting here at the school as soon as possible. We have got to get a handle on these problems."

"Uh, Mrs. Todd, my husband and I are divorced and I have no idea what problems you're talking about. I've been meaning to call and check on things at school but I haven't gotten around to it yet. What type of problems are we talking about?"

"I didn't realize you and your husband were divorced. Perhaps that is part of the problem. Sean has been acting out in class for several weeks and not doing his work. It has been getting worse. Today he called another student a very filthy name. It has to come to a stop."

"Why haven't I been informed about these problems if they have been going on for a while?"

"Mrs. Alexander, we have sent home reports several times. I have been requesting a meeting with you."

"I haven't received anything. How did you send them?"

"They were given to Sean for him to give to you. Are you saying he hasn't given them to you?"

"No he hasn't. But why would you expect him to, if it was going to get him in trouble. Never mind, I'll deal with that later. Would it be okay if I met with you tomorrow morning at ten?"

"Yes, that would be fine."

"Okay, and if you don't mind, don't tell Sean about the meeting. I want to see if he'll tell me anything on his own tonight. Will he be in the meeting tomorrow?"

"I think it would be best but that's up to you. And I'll tell his teacher not to say anything about it either. I'll arrange for someone to stay in her class so she can attend the meeting. I look forward to seeing you tomorrow."

The rest of Amy's day was a blur to her. She could not imagine what type of problems Sean was having, or creating, and what filthy name he would have called someone. It was not like he was hearing bad language at home or in the homes of any friends. When she got home, Marshall was in his room doing his homework. He had a big test to take in a couple of weeks and had been diligently studying for it. Sean was playing video games, as usual. Sarah was on the telephone with someone making wedding arrangements. Amy was grateful for her mother's assistance, coming to the house to stay with the boys until she came home from work. She supposed that may change with her mother's pending marriage.

Amy started supper, going through the motions with her mind on other things. She was so engrossed with her thoughts she didn't hear her mother enter the kitchen. When she spoke to her, Amy nearly dropped the pot of spaghetti.

"Well, I found a caterer. Shirley's said they can have everything including the cakes ready, even though it's short notice. I've never used them before but I've heard they're good. I certainly hope so."

"Mom, speaking of the wedding, after you're married are you still going to be able to come over and stay with the boys? I know Marshall would be okay on his own but not Sean, even with Marshall in the house. If not, I guess I'll have to find an after school program for him."

"Loren and I have already talked about it. I plan to continue coming over until Sean is a little older. Loren said he had a bad experience with one of his grandkids attending a day care and he feels it would be best if Sean is in the care of family. But you may end up having us over for dinner frequently. Loren loves children and he is looking forward to having an extended family. Besides, I think it would be a fair trade off for him having to wait for his dinner."

"I don't mind you two coming for dinner but you may have to help me a little. I'm not the cook you are. I want to ask you something. Sean's principal called me at work today. She said Sean has been having problems at school and just today used some pretty bad language. Have you heard anything like that from him or seen some papers from the school?"

"No, I haven't. But he usually comes in and goes straight to his room and closes the door. I know he changes clothes but I suppose if he is bringing home papers from school he could be hiding them. Do you ever go through his backpack?"

"I never thought I needed to. Mrs. Todd indicated that it could be a recent development and possibly a result of the divorce. I'm going to try to get him to talk at dinner. Just play along with me."

Amy called both boys to dinner and as they ate she asked them about school. Marshall said his assignment was going well and should be completed before the deadline. He was expecting his grades to be about the same as usual, mostly As. Sean said school was okay, which had become his usual comment. Amy asked if he was having any problems. He replied he wasn't but he didn't like second grade.

"You're not the only one," Amy told her son. "One of my customers has a son in the second grade and he is having some problems. His grades went down and he got in trouble at school. Instead of bringing home a note from his teacher, he hid it. His mother didn't know anything about what was going on at school so she didn't know he needed any help. It's sad because he could end up failing second grade. I know you boys wouldn't do anything like that, would you?"

"It wouldn't do any good to hide that from you because the principal would call you eventually and that would just make things worse. We'd end up getting in more trouble than if we had been honest," Marshall said.

Amy wondered if Marshall had figured out what was up. She looked at Sean. "What about you, son?" she asked him.

With big eyes, he said, "No, Mom. I wouldn't do that. Would the principal really call you?"

"I'm sure she would, eventually. I would hope that you wouldn't hide anything from me though. How can I help if I don't know there is a problem?"

As they cleared the table, Sean looked guilty and fearful. Amy wondered if he would come clean or wait to see if the principal would call. He headed to his room as soon as he had put his dishes away. Amy had to call him back to the living room to put his games away. He hung his head and quickly did as he was told.

"Well, maybe I have a bigger problem than I thought," Amy said to her mother as he left the room.

"Children will test their parents. He needs to find out what his limits are, how you will react to the things he does. A lot of parents in your situation will let them get by with things because they feel the child has been hurt by the divorce. Sean has no reason to feel that way and you know it. He has not been hurt. But with Brandon gone, he may also feel he has no reason to fear your punishment. Brandon was always the one he was afraid of. What are you gong to do?" Sarah asked.

"I'm not sure. I don't know what all he's done at school. I know he's used some bad language and has been hiding notes from school but that is all I know. I hate to have to spank him but I may have to. I guess I'll take his video games away. That usually makes him angry though. I just don't know."

After Sarah left that evening, Amy thought about Sean's acting up at school. She had had some problems at home but didn't think they had also been occurring at school. Single parenting was difficult and she was just now finding out how difficult. She had a fear this may just be the beginning. The next morning Amy meet with Mrs. Todd and Sean's teacher, Linda Savage. Sean looked like he was gong to be fed to the lions. Perhaps she should have told him about the call from his principal. As they entered the principal's office, Mrs. Todd began to outline Sean's activities at school.

"I don't know what is going on in your home but Sean has displayed some pretty poor behavior for several weeks. On the playground and in the lunch room he has been mean to some other students. He is hitting and calling them names. He even spit in one child's lunch. He has had to stay in at recess to do extra work as punishment," Mrs. Todd said.

Mrs. Savage took up where she left off. "Sean has not been turning in his class work and refused to take his spelling test for the past two weeks. He has been disruptive and won't stay in his seat. He talks while I'm giving the lessons. Yesterday he called a little girl a very filthy name. And it was completely unprovoked. I don't know what to do with him."

Amy looked at her son. She was shocked at the report.

"Sean, what do you have to say about this?" she asked.

"Nothing," he replied sullenly.

"Nothing? I think you better come up with something."

Sean looked away and didn't reply. Mrs. Todd suggested that he wait in the outer office while the adults finished talking. He got up and walked out of the room.

"Mrs. Alexander, I don't want to pry but what type of problems are there in the home? Things that he would be angry about?" Mrs. Todd asked.

"Nothing. Really. His father and I have been divorced for several months. Before he left things were more difficult. His dad was the angry one but I tried to keep the boys away from him so his anger wouldn't spill over on them. And I don't have a clue where he could be hearing any bad language. I really don't know what is going on with him."

"I'm going to have the counselor visit with him a couple of times a week. He may just be testing us or there may be a serious problem here. What do you plan to do at home?"

"I'm going to try to get him to talk with me. He always has in the past. But I'm going to have to punish him, I can't let this go. If he's testing me, he has to know that there will be punishment for breaking the rules."

"Well, keep us informed so we can help and we will do the same. Thank you for taking the time to come in. In the future I will call instead of sending a note home with Sean."

"Thank you," Amy said, as she headed for the door.

Sean didn't look at her as she came to stand before him. She took his face in her hand and forced him to look at her.

"Do not sit down to play any games or watch any T.V. when you get home today. When I get home I want to find you doing homework. If you don't have any homework, I want you working on your math facts. Do you understand me? I will tell Gram what I'm telling you so she will know what you're supposed to be doing. After dinner, you and I are going to have a long talk. So you better be thinking about what you have to say about all of this."

When Amy got back to work, her boss asked how the meeting had gone. She told him what had happened and that she was clueless about what to do about it. He told her his son had done the same thing. He warned her not to act in anger as he had done, that didn't solve anything. But he assured her that she was a good mother and was smart enough to do the right thing. Everything would eventually be okay. Even his son had turned out fine, he said, as he reached over and lightly punched his now grown child in the arm affectionately. Amy certainly hoped so.

She called her mother and told her what she had told Sean. Sarah was willing to see to it that Sean did as he was told. She too would try to get him to talk. Later that day when the boys came in, Sarah sent Sean to the dining table to get to work. She went to Marshall's room to talk to him about his brother. She briefly explained to him what had transpired at school.

"Do you have any idea what's going on with Sean? Has he said anything to you about how he feels?" Sarah asked.

"The only thing he's said is that he's glad Dad's gone. I don't see why that would make him act up. Maybe he thinks Mom won't punish him. Dad always did that, you know. If she doesn't punish him, it's only going to get worse," Marshall said.

When Amy came home that evening, Sean was still sitting at the table. Sarah told her what Marshall had said before she left.

Amy sat down at the table and looked at Sean. He looked back but said nothing.

"Sean, what's going on? Why are you misbehaving?" she asked.

"I don't know," he said.

"Well, we're going to have to find out. In the mean time you're going to have to be punished. I'm going to put your games up and you can't have them back until I get good reports for two straight weeks. If things don't change you won't get them back at all."

"That's not fair! You're always being mean to me. You're never mean to Marshall. He's always the best. He's the only one you love."

Sean's anger was explosive. He swiped the books off the table and kicked one across the room. Amy grabbed him by the arm before he could run from the room.

"That is not true and you know it. The only reason you get punished is because you have misbehaved. If you're jealous of your brother perhaps you should try to misbehave less. I do not treat you any different than I do him. He just gives me less reason to punish him. Now pick up these books and sit back down. We're not through with this conversation. I want to know where you are picking up bad language."

Sean did as he was told, although somewhat grudgingly.

"I heard Dad call you that when you were fighting."

"When did you hear your dad say stuff like that?"

"It's true, Mom," Marshall interjected, though Amy had not known he had come into the room. "We used to hear Dad say all kinds of ugly stuff. I know you had your door shut but Dad yelled pretty loud. Sean, you can't talk like that. People will think we're all trashy if you go around talking dirty. I know Mom won't appreciate you giving us a bad reputation. It's bad enough with the things Dad did. But I won't appreciate it either. You can be jealous all you want of me but one day if you keep being bad, I won't want you hanging around me. I'll be embarrassed for people to know you're my brother."

With that Marshall left the room. Amy could see his words hurt Sean.

"Do you see that even though you do something, it reflects on other people. Your actions will effect Marshall and me also. Even Gram. I know you're not a bad kid. Something's bothering you. Why don't you tell me about it."

Sean's eyes pooled with tears but he didn't say anything. He just sat there looking dejected. Amy pulled him to her and hugged him tight. She felt him crying but he wouldn't say anything. She kissed him on his forehead and told him to keep working while she fixed supper. He went to bed that night without ever opening up to his mother.

Chapter Seven

Amy watched her troubled son the next few weeks for some sign that would indicate what was troubling him. She could see in his face strain and sadness but he would not say what was on his mind. She called the school to see if perhaps the counselor had learned anything during their meetings.

"Mrs. Whitten, this is Amy Alexander, Sean's mother. I'm concerned about Sean. He hasn't had any more incidences that I know of at school, and his demeanor at home has been somewhat subdued, but I am clueless about what is going on with him. Has he said anything, is there anything I need to be aware of?"

"He's very quiet when he comes to my office. He rarely says anything at all unless he's answering a question and then it's usually a yes or no answer. I have asked him if he's having problems at home, if he is angry at a parent or sibling or afraid of something. He says he isn't. There are some things I would like to know about the home environment. You and your husband are divorced, correct?"

"Yes, that's correct. Brandon and I divorced about three months ago. But he had already moved out of the house before that. He had been gone for about three months before we filed for divorce."

Deirdre Kelley

"What was the relationship between Sean and his father?"

"There wasn't much of a relationship between them. Even before Brandon left, he stayed away from the house a great deal. He wasn't involved in anything they did. When he was home, he was often angry and they stayed in their rooms to avoid him. I can't see that the divorce would affect him negatively. I would think Sean would feel better since his dad left."

"Perhaps. What about your relationship with him? Has it changed any? And isn't there another child in the house? What is their relationship like?"

"I have an older son who is fifteen. I have always felt that I had a good relationship with both boys and they have always had a good relationship with each other. Marshall is a good student in school, makes good grades and doesn't get in any trouble. Sean has voiced what I guess is some jealously about the fact that Marshall is loved more than him and gets to do more but that's not true. Marshall just doesn't give me any trouble. He does what he's told to do and helps out around the house. He does his homework without any prompting. I tried explaining that to Sean on numerous occasions, that if he would behave he would get to do more and be grounded less. But it hasn't done much good. It's hard to say what kind of relationship we have with Sean right now because he hasn't interacted with us much lately. But before it was good. We played games and did things as a family, just the three of us, and sometimes my mother."

"The next time he comes in for his visit I'll ask him about his brother. If I can find an area that he feels comfortable talking about maybe it will help him to get comfortable and open up in other areas. I'll let you know if I find out anything. Thanks for calling."

Amy wasn't sure that the counselor would be able to help. Sean had really receded lately. She was afraid she was going to lose him. Her planned outing with the two boys had been put on hold until after the wedding. Marshall was involved in a school project and her mother's wedding plans seemed to consume her, though she wasn't sure why. Amy decided that she and Sean would do something together on a smaller scale. Maybe they could reconnect.

That evening when she got home he was in his room just laying on his bed as he now so often did. He had seemed to lose interest in his video games, and though under other circumstances Amy would have been glad, now it concerned her.

"Sean, are you okay?" she asked, brushing his hair from his forehead.

"I'm fine," he replied quietly.

"Well, if you feel okay, I was wondering since it's a Friday night and you don't have to be up early tomorrow for school, if you wanted to go a movie and dinner with me."

"I don't know. What are we going to see?"

"I have no idea. I don't even know what good movies are playing. You decide on the movie and I decide on the dinner. How's that?"

"I can decide on the movie? Any movie?" he said, setting up and looking interested.

"Yep, any movie."

"Okay, let's go."

Amy was trilled to see Sean excited and more like his old self. She told Marshall where they were going and if he needed anything to call his grandmother. He told them to have a good time and winked at her as she was leaving the room. She again wondered at Marshall's perceptiveness.

Amy got to the theater just as the movie Sean wanted to see was starting. She sat through mutant metamorphosis and good mutant verses bad mutant and wondered what kind of mind thought up such stuff. Amy thought the movie pointless and the special effects way overdone but Sean gave it rave reviews. She was glad to see him smiling and laughing again. Amy decided Mexican food would be on the menu for the evening because she knew how much Sean loved cheese dip and chips. He chatted about the movie for a while, between stuffing his mouth with the chips. By the time dinner had arrived, he grew quiet and pensive and Amy wondered why the change.

"Mom, you know Carlie goes to visit her dad sometimes? She said one time that they went on vacation with her grandma and grandpa. That's her dad's mom and dad. She also goes on vacation with her other grandma and grandpa. How come we don't have a grandpa? We got a grandma," Sean suddenly asked.

"Well, my dad died a while back before you were born. And your dad's dad died when he was a little boy. His mom got married again, like your gram is going to do soon, but your dad wasn't very close to his mom's husband so even though he's kind of like a grandpa because he's married to your grandma, he...."

"He doesn't want to be our grandpa," Sean finished for his mother.

"That's about right," she said. "But when Gram and Loren get married, he will be happy to be your grandpa."

"I know, we talked about it. He said we could call him Grandpa or Loren, what ever we wanted. Marshall and I talked about and we agreed to call him Granddad. Marshall said it would make him feel like he was part of our family and it would make Gram happy too."

"I'm glad you made that decision. It's hard being part of a family when the family was a family before you came along, like coming in in the middle of a movie and not knowing what's going on. That's real grown up thinking, Sean. Gram will really be pleased."

After a few minutes of silence, Sean had another question.

"How come Dad's mom's husband didn't like Dad. He was just a little boy, right? Did Dad do something to make him not like him?"

"Not that I know of. Your dad was about five, I think, when his dad died. His mom got married again not long after that. But the man just didn't like kids, I guess. Some people are like that. They don't have any reason for not liking kids, but they just don't. It may be because they are selfish or jealous and want all the attention for themselves. I don't know. I never met him. All I know about him is what your dad told me about him."

"Was he mean to Dad? Is that why Dad was mean, because someone was mean to him?"

Amy was a bit astonished at this bit of reasoning from her young son.

"I don't know, son. Maybe. Your dad didn't talk much about when he was growing up so I suppose that could be what happened. I know sometimes adults copy the actions that they learn from their parents. Even though that was not his dad, he lived in the same house with him for a long time. You're a pretty smart kid, you know. I hadn't thought of that. I wondered why your dad was the way he was and couldn't figure out any answers. I thought it was because he didn't like me."

"Why would you think he didn't like you? I thought it was because he didn't like me. I made messes and noise and broke things. He was always yelling at me, telling me I was stupid. I thought he hit you because you wouldn't let him hit me. I hated him because he hit you. How come he didn't like me? I tried to be a good kid. I tried not to make messes and noise. I tried to do good in school but it's hard for me. I didn't want to be stupid. I tried Mom, I really did. I'm sorry Dad hit you because of me. I'm sorry."

Amy was stunned. Tears poured down Sean's face and she was fighting to catch her breath after his outburst. She reached around the table and pulled him close to her. Amy laid some money on the table to pay her bill and ushered her son from the restaurant. She opened the door of the car and setting him in the seat, she bent to his level.

"Sean, whatever made your dad do the things he did had nothing to do you or the things you did. It had nothing to do with me or the things I did. You were a normal little boy. All little boys make messes and noise. They break things. There is nothing wrong with that unless they do it to be mean. But you didn't, you were just growing up. You are a good and wonderful child. You are not stupid. You are bright and intelligent. Your father was angry about something that had nothing to do with us but took it out on us. It's like being mad at a kid at school and yelling at Marshall. He's not the one you're mad at but the one you yell at.

"He doesn't know why you're yelling at him because he didn't do anything wrong. And I would much rather your father hit me than you. I don't blame you for anything. I love you so much, son. I know you tried to be good but we could never be good enough for your dad. I was so afraid he would really hurt you when he was angry. I'm sorry I didn't make him leave long before he did. I'm the one that owes you an apology."

Amy held her tearful son close and prayed he would understand. She did not want him to think he was to blame for his father's abuse. Sean pushed her away and took her face in his hands as she had so often done to his.

"Mom, you didn't do anything wrong. You were just trying to do your best. We just got to pray for Dad, right, for God to heal his heart? And we got to pray so we don't be like him, right?"

"Right. That's what we have to do," Amy said through her own tears.

As she got in the car and pulled out of the parking lot she wondered if this was what had been disturbing Sean these past weeks. Perhaps they could work through this and get things back on an even keel. She desperately hoped so. Later that evening as she related the conversation with her mother, she could her the tears in her mother's voice.

"Well, Amy, I hope the problem is behind us. But don't put your guard down. This may be just one hurdle you have to pass," Sarah said.

"I know but I can hope. The counselor seems to think it has something to do with the divorce, though I don't know why. I suppose it has to do with the timing of his problems. Please keep this at the top of your prayer list. By the way, he told me that he and Marshall have decided Loren is Granddad."

"Oh, Loren will be so pleased. He really likes the boys. I have to admit that as we get closer to the wedding date, I'm getting a bit nervous. I don't know why though. Everything is coming along so well. I'll be glad when it's all behind me."

"Three more weeks. Has Loren told you where he's taking you on your honeymoon yet?"

"No, he hasn't. I told him I needed to know so I would know what to pack. He said to pack for any contingency, from a bikini to a snowsuit. Then he laughed. He said include a swimsuit and evening wear. Other than that he said whatever was comfortable would do. I told him I don't own any evening wear and he told me to get some. I don't even know what evening wear is but I guess I'm going to learn. Want to go shopping tomorrow with me?"

Amy was tickled at Loren's handling of the honeymoon. She knew he was taking her mother on a cruise. She should go with her mother for the shopping since she knew where they would be heading.

"Sure, I'll go. Mind if the boys tag along? We can go to the mall and they can go to the video arcade while we shop."

"Sound like a date. See you tomorrow."

Chapter Eight

As Amy stood at the front of the church, butterflies churned her stomach and it wasn't even her wedding. She could imagine her mother's knees were ready to buckle. But she strode beautifully down the isle on the arm of her son. Kevin gave his mother's hand to Loren and the preacher tied the couple together after hearing their vows. Amy heard the words, heard the declaration between the couple pledging to love, honor and cherish each other until death parted them. However, the image in Amy's head was when she herself had stood and pledged to honor the same vows. Pangs of self-pity took her breath away as she watched her mother marry a man who was obviously in love with her.

"I'm a good person," she thought to herself. "Is there something about me that makes me unworthy of that kind of love? Why can't I be loved like that?"

She took a deep breath and pushed the thoughts away. Her mother deserved this, she had waited a long time for her turn at love. Amy was determined to be happy and not wallow in self pity. God was in control and He knew what was best for her. She would have to believe in Him to lead where He would in her life. By the time the bride and groom strode back down the isle, Amy was ready to wilt. She could not imagine doing this again herself. She didn't think another marriage could be in her future. The reception was fun and Loren's family mixed well with her own. Amy felt that the union of the two families was going to be a wonderful blessing.

Amy looked at Marshall and realized that with the magic sixteenth birthday around the corner, he was growing up. He looked ever bit of a man in his tux. She noticed several young ladies giving him the eye. One in particular got a return glance from Marshall. Amy didn't recognize her so she thought the girl must be a friend or relative of Loren's family. Sensing someone near her, she turned and saw Greg Jansen standing slightly behind her and looking at the same girl.

"Hello, Greg. I was noticing the girl standing over there. I don't recognize her," Amy said.

"That's my daughter, Alyssa," he said.

"Oh. I didn't know your daughter was here."

Amy had learned that Greg's wife and children had stayed behind when he moved to town with his job until he had gotten settled in. She supposed he was settled in so it was reasonable for his family to be with him now. She had not met either his wife or his children yet.

"Evelyn and the kids got here about two weeks ago. Alyssa has been a little reluctant to come to church. It appears she has an acquaintance, however, so perhaps it will be a little easier to get her in church this Sunday," he said nodding toward Marshall.

"How would they know each other?" she asked.

"School most likely. Alyssa is in the eleventh grade. Isn't that what grade Marshall is in?"

"Yes, he is. What about your wife and son?"

"Evelyn will come when Alyssa comes. Dillon, well at nineteen who knows. His approach to Christianity is exploratory. He is one of those logical types. True faith is not his strong point. He wants positive proof but he has not closed his mind to it. I'm afraid it's going to take something powerful to change him. Alyssa is very deep with her Christianity. It's at the core of her being. But she's very shy and that's why she's been reluctant to come to church."

"Marshall takes his faith very seriously. I'm thankful for that. So many kids that grow up in church take it all for granted and never make a personal commitment or simply cast it aside for the things of this world. They think they're missing something by being a Christian."

"I felt like that for a long time. I wanted to have all the glitter the world offered because I thought it would give me security and satisfaction. But no matter what I achieved or gained, it didn't make me feel like what I thought it would. When my mother was diagnosed with cancer it was her faith that gave her the strength to endure her treatments and overcome it. She never gave up, she never complained. She said God would never put more on her than she could handle. I disagreed, I thought it was more than anyone could endure. But she said God knew what was best and even if He took her home she would praise Him for His goodness. How do you resist that kind of faith? I wanted what she had. I wanted that kind of hope," Greg said.

"I grew up in church but, like you said, never made a personal commitment. Sitting beside my mother's bed, listening to her tell me about her loving God, I made a commitment to Him and He has not disappointed me. There have been rough times. Evelyn wasn't too excited about my choice and for a while it looked like we weren't going to make it. That's when Alyssa came along. Evelyn almost lost her several times and she told me later that she told God if He let her have this baby, she'd raise her in church. She has kept her promise and Alyssa has devoted her heart to God. Dillon never let it get too deep, he had only a surface Christianity. I think it's more out of fear, like God will ask to much of him and he come up short. I worry that one day it may be too late for him to see the truth that is so blindingly clear to me," he continued.

Amy looked at the seemingly shy girl standing a little apart from the others. As she watched she saw Marshall approach the girl and began speaking to her. Her heart squeezed at the thought of Marshall being a tool used by God to draw others into His house. As the girl looked up at Marshall, another thought caused her heart to squeeze, she herself had been only sixteen when she had first met Brandon.

The bride and groom began to make their departure from the reception. Sean ran up to her and handed her a bottle of bubbles.

"We're going to blow bubbles at Gram and Granddad when they get in the car. And you should see what Uncle Kevin and the others did to Granddad's car. They wrote all over it with shoe polish and filled it full of balloons. They won't even be able to get in the car," Sean said gleefully.

Sure enough the car was full of balloons. As Loren opened the door for Sarah, they spilled out. Sarah began scooping them out so she could get in. Finally the couple was off for the first part of their honeymoon, the real one to began after the Christmas holidays. Amy headed back inside to begin cleaning up. She caught sight of Marshall and Alyssa again, sitting in a remote corner talking. Sean stayed outside with some of the other kids, stomping the balloons to make them pop. As she began clearing the tables, she noticed her new step-sister-in-law, Morgan working at another table.

"Well, now that the kids are off we can relax," Morgan said with a laugh.

"Yes and I'm ready. I feel like I was preparing for my own wedding," Amy said.

"Me too. I was wondering something. Where are they going to live? I mean both of them have a house, which one are they going to live in?" Morgan asked.

"You know, I don't know. I hadn't even thought of that. Both houses are nice and in good neighborhoods. It'd be a hard choice."

The women finished cleaning up and Amy gathered her sons and headed home. She wanted to ask Marshall about Alyssa but didn't want to do it in front of Sean. After changing clothes, Sean went out to ride his bike. Marshall headed for the phone.

"Oh, I wanted to ask you something," Amy said.

"What is it?" Marshall asked.

"Well, it can wait until you make your call."

"It may be a while. What is you want to ask?"

"I was talking to Alyssa's father after the wedding. I didn't realize that she was here now. Have you met her at school?"

"Yeah but I don't have any classes with her. We do have the same lunch period but I haven't seen her at lunch. I was just going to call her and see if she wanted to meet me at school after the Christmas holidays so I could introduce her around."

"Or you could ask her at church tomorrow. That is if she comes. Her dad said she is pretty shy and he was hoping since she knew you she might start coming to church with him."

"Yeah, that'd be nice. I'm going to call her and see if she is coming to church. Is there anything else?"

"No, I guess not," Amy told her son's departing back.

She went to her own room and shut the door. She was feeling somewhat depressed in the aftermath of the wedding and in her son's sudden attention outside the family. She was not sure she was ready for him to grow up. She thought about what might lie ahead for her. In a year and a half

Marshall would be preparing for college. His plans would take him out of the state and she knew she would miss him greatly when he left. She still had a few years left with Sean but those years would undoubtedly pass quickly. As she pondered her future, the door bell rang. Opening the door she found Lydia standing there with a huge tub of ice cream.

"Got some spoons?" she asked with a goofy grin.

"Sure. Come on in." Amy said, trying to figure out what Lydia was up to.

Amy got two spoons and they sat down at the dinning table. "I thought this might be an ice cream kind of afternoon. Sometimes weddings bring me down, thought they might do the same to you. How are you doing?" Lydia asked.

"Okay, I guess. How are you?"

"Troubled. Worried. Scared," Lydia replied, around a mouth full of ice cream.

"Why? Why would my mother's wedding make you feel like that?"

"Amy, have you thought about getting married again?"

"No and I don't want to."

"Why not? Don't you want to get married again?"

"Nope."

"Come on, really? I do. Why don't you?"

"Because I failed so badly in my first marriage. It was a disaster and I don't want to repeat any of it."

"You did not fail in your marriage. Sure it was a disaster but not because of you. Why did you think you failed?"

"I don't know. I guess I just wasn't a good wife."

"In what way? What is a good wife?"

"I don't know, a helpmate like the Bible says."

"Okay. What is a bad wife?"

"A bad wife? Someone who doesn't take care of her house, her kids, her husband. Someone who doesn't care about meeting their needs but only seeks to please herself.

I don't know. A woman who cheats on her husband, spends the utility money on herself instead of paying the bills, lets her kids go to school dirty and hungry because she's too lazy to do what's right, lives like a pig. It could be a lot of things."

"Right. And which of those things are you guilty of? None of them. You are a great mother to your children and you were a great wife to Brandon. Your marriage failed because he was a poor husband."

"Maybe. But who's to say that I won't end up in another situation just like the one I came out of. I have no trust left, Lydia. If I can't trust my partner, what do I have to base a relationship on?"

"I agree with you. Which is why I'm scared. I want to feel what I saw in your mother's eyes. I want to love again and to be loved. Carl and I had a good relationship. I wrecked it by not paying him the attention he deserved. Talk about being self centered. I was totally absorbed in my job when I became manager of the restaurant. I had worked so hard to get there. And when Carlie was born, I could only see her. She was my entire life. I was even jealous when Carl held his own daughter. I wanted to be holding her. And you know what, they love each other in spite of my trying to keep them apart. But it was after Carl left that I realized what I had done and what I had lost. And I know that I want to have that again. But I don't want to jump at the first relationship that opens up to me and it be the wrong one. That's what scares me, that I won't wait to be sure. I hope you don't close the door on marriage just because of what you went through with Brandon."

"I guess we'll have to see what happens down the road. It's really too soon for me to even consider it now. I have to be at peace with myself and I haven't got there yet. But thanks for the lecture. And thanks for the ice cream."

Chapter Nine

Two days later, after she had repeatedly slapped both Marshall's and Sean's hands out of the cherries, Amy finished the pineapple upside down cake and the potato salad for Christmas dinner the next day. As she sat finishing her gift wrapping that evening, she thought about the difference between this Christmas and last year's. She was glad that her mother's wedding had occupied her mind before the holidays. She had not had much time to think about this first Christmas as a divorced woman. Amy wasn't sure why it made a difference.

It was not as if Brandon had been very involved with them during the holidays. He made a brief appearance for dinner and gift opening then disappeared. She was always embarrassed by his behavior even though it had come to be expected. This year she wouldn't have to make any explanations for his disappearance. She should feel relieved but she found that instead she felt embarrassed just as before but for another reason. She wondered how long she would feel like she had committed a crime and was a marked person, as if a stain was evidenced on her because of some guilt, though she had not done anything wrong. She knew it was irrational to feel that way but she couldn't get past it for some reason. She prayed about it constantly but continued to feel guilty and dirty.

As she crawled into bed, she fought back tears. Why did she have to feel guilty for what her husband had done? He had abandoned his family, committed adultery and sold his self-respect for drugs. Why did she feel like everyone looked down on her for that? Where was the peace that she had felt months ago? The tears could no longer be held back. They streamed down her face, soaking into her pillow.

"God, why am I feeling like this? Why can't I find peace? Brandon sinned against you and his family and yet

I'm feeling guilty like I did something wrong. I'm the one struggling and try to keep things running as smoothly as I can for the boys. What is you would have me do? I want to do what you would have me do, to live as you would have me live. I know you love me and care for me but I need to feel your presence in my life. I need to know you hold my hand. I need to feel like you have forgiven my for what ever my part was in the failure of my marriage. I need to know that everything is okay between you and I, that I'm not missing something. Lead me, show me what it is I need to know to move on, to feel your presence again. Please, God, please," she sobbed.

As she lay there, wiping the tears from her face, she almost missed it. That voice in her head, the one she longed to hear, whispered "Worship me." That was all. It didn't really make sense. She knew that as a Christian she was to worship God. And she thought she did. She sang during song service at church and with her CDs around the house. She drifted off to sleep with this on her mind.

The next day the Christmas celebration took her mind from the whispered words the night before. It was quite the celebration with the new family members there to join in. Sarah and Loren had decided to leave on their honeymoon after Christmas. Amy was glad. She and the boys had a great time with Loren's family. That evening as they got back home, Marshall headed for the phone.

"Are you going to call your girlfriend again?" teased Sean.

Marshall playfully batted him with the phone before shutting himself inside his room. Sean settled himself to play a new game he had gotten for Christmas. Amy curled in a chair and looked at the journal her mother had given her for Christmas. The blank pages both lured her and scared her. She had kept a journal as a young girl, giving it up after her marriage to Brandon. She wasn't sure why she had quit keeping a journal but perhaps it was time to began again. The words came back to her then. Worship me, He said. She closed her eyes and let her mind go.

"Lord, you know I worship you. I adore you. You are my hope. But I don't understand. Please, help me to understand," she breathed silently.

She sat meditating on God and what it meant to her to know him and have her hope in him. And just as the words had come the night before, the answer came in the same quiet whisper.

"Worship me. Know that I love you and want to be in communion with you. I see the hurts and wounds of my people, even the ones they inflict on each other. It breaks my heart. Your worship lifts my heart and spirit just as it does yours. Your worship is that communion, that connection that bridges the distance between us. Look to me for your answers. Look to me for your peace. I will never leave you nor forsake you, my child."

While it was not the direct answer she would have preferred, Amy thought she understood. She knew worship was adoration, a single mindedness with the focus on God. She had become so focused on how she was feeling, the doubts and fears, she thought little of much else. She knew things could have been much worse for her and the boys. She was blessed that it was not nearly as bad as it could have been. She and the boys had not been seriously hurt by Brandon. His punishment to the boys was always hard but he never crossed the line. His abuse was directed mainly at her. And even that was all behind them now. She should be praising God for his blessings instead of bemoaning her situation.

She remembered the passage in Jeremiah where God told his people He knew the thoughts of peace He had for them, to give them a future and a hope. She also remembered it was followed by saying if his people called on Him, He would listen. If we sought Him, we would find Him if we searched with all our hearts. Amy thought that was perhaps her problem, she did not seek Him with all her heart. She held part of herself back. She clung to her wounds like badges of honor. And she had let her imagined wounds distract her from focusing on God and his promises.

"Mom," Marshal said, shaking her out of her reverie.

"What?" Amy responded, blinking her eyes open.

"Can I talk to you," he asked.

"What is it?"

"While I was on the phone with Alyssa, Dad called."

"What'd he want?" she asked, suddenly alarmed.

"I don't know, he kind of rambled. I think he was high or something. He wanted to know if I had any money. I told him no and he hung up."

"Well, if he calls back, ever, let me talk to him," she directed her son.

"No problem," he said, heading back to his room.

Brandon made good money at his job but if he was heavy into drugs it was conceivable that he could be spending it faster than he was making it. Amy didn't know if this was a new development in Brandon's life or if it was just part of his holiday celebration. She looked at the journal she still held in her hands and thought about the journey she had already traveled. What still lie ahead, she wondered. She had to go back to work the next day and Marshall was going to keep an eye on Sean for the next three days while she worked. Her mother would be back from her honeymoon by the starting of the school week to watch him after school. She was worried that Sean would not behave for Marshall while she was away. She had talked to him about it and he had promised to be good. She certainly hoped so.

She got her clothes ready for work and sent the boys to bed. The next day at work went smooth, mostly due to the fact that people were still busy with friends and family and had no time for repairs. She was able to get a little caught up on some of the correspondence and filing that needed to be done. The day passed swiftly and she was heading home when her cell phone rang, distracting her from yelling at the crazy person who had decided to pull out in front of her nearly causing her to hit his vehicle.

"Hello," she answered abruptly.

"Mom, he called again," Marshall said. "Sean answered the phone."

It took her a moment to figure out who "he" was. "Well, did Sean tell you what his dad said to him?"

"No but what ever it was scared him. He's in his room crying."

"I'll be home in a minute. Don't let him answer the phone again."

Amy wasn't sure if she should be scared or angry. What could Brandon want? Why was he suddenly calling her house? They had not heard anything from him since he left. As she pulled up in the driveway, she saw Marshall peek out the front window. She guessed he was a little worried himself.

"Did he say anything," she asked Marshall as she got into the house. He locked the door behind her.

"He said Dad said something about getting rid of us. He said he sounded crazy. I figure he was probably high like last night and he's just talking out of his head. That's what I told Sean, that he was just talking crazy and wouldn't do anything. But Sean's pretty scared."

"Well, I guess leaving you two alone this week is not the best idea. We'll have to make some other plans. I need to talk to Sean."

Amy went to his door and knocked. The door was locked. "Sean, it's Mom. Can I come in?"

The door was unlocked and Sean's face peered through the crack. It was tear streaked and his eyes looked frightened.

"Sweetheart. Mom's not going to let anything happen to you," she told her son as she pulled him close. "Tell me what he said to you."

"He asked where you were and I told him you were at work. He asked if you had any money laying around the house and I told him no. He said you were taking all his money and he ought to get rid of us. Then he hung up," Sean said as he clung to his mother.

"Well, I'm sure he didn't mean it. But just to be sure how about we plan on you and Marshall staying somewhere else the rest of the week?"

Sean nodded his head, looking a little relieved. Now all Amy had to do is figure out where they could stay on such notice. In the end, it was decided that they would go to Lydia's. Sean would go with Carlie to her sitter and Marshall would go to work with Lydia. He could help out and perhaps earn a little money. Amy was relieved with the situation. She kept going to the phone to call her mother and then remembering she was on a cruse ship in the ocean somewhere. They made it to Friday without another troubling phone call from Brandon. Amy had just begun to believe that the worst was over when the call she was dreading came.

Snatching up the phone before either of the boys could get it, she said, "Hello."

"Amy! I've been trying to get in touch with you. I need some money," Brandon said. His voice didn't indicate he was high but it sounded desperate.

"I don't have any money," Amy told him as she ducked into her room and shut the door.

"I know you do. You get a check every other week for child support. I need some of that money. I need it now."

Deirdre Kelley

"I don't have any money. It takes all I make and the child support to make ends meet. And I haven't gotten a child support check in three weeks. What happened to your job?"

"I got fired. So you better not bank on any more money from me. You're on your own now."

"How am I supposed to make it without that money?"

"I don't know and I don't care. It's not my problem. You can let the house go and make Marshall get a job. He should be old enough to get a job."

"It would be more expensive to let the house go than to keep it. Besides, it would be unfair to uproot the boys after what you have already put them through. It's not Marshall responsibility to support us, it's yours. How about you get a job?"

"I don't need a job. I need money, fast money. And you've been in my way of having it. I can make those boys disappear, you know."

"Are you threatening the safety of your sons? If anything happens to either one of them, you will be the first person the police will look for, I'll make sure of it. Don't you ever make the mistake of hurting my children…" Amy was saying as the line went dead.

She stood there shaking, unsure of what to do. She decided that perhaps the best thing to do was get out of the house. As she opened her door, she bumped into Marshall. He had been listening to her side of the phone call.

"What's going on?" he asked.

"I don't know. But I think we are going to stay at Mom's for the night. She and Loren won't be home until Sunday, so it'll be okay. Tomorrow we can make some plans. Go pack a few things and I'll talk to Sean."

As Amy and the boys gathered some clothing and drove the few houses down to her mother's place, she wondered what her next move should be. She didn't know if the drugs were talking or if he was desperate enough to really pull some stupid stunt that could put her and the boys in jeopardy.

Chapter Ten

The weekend passed uneventfully. Amy had forwarded her phone calls to her mother's house and contacted the police department. She had explained what she thought the situation most likely was, though she was not entirely sure what it was. Unfortunately she didn't have an address for Brandon. He had been staying with his girlfriend but his call on Friday had come from a pay phone. She could hear the sounds of vehicles as they passed where ever he had made the call from. She felt better after talking to the police because if something did happen, they would have a record of her report. Her mother and step-father returned home Sunday afternoon looking absolutely wonderful. Amy explained what had happened and why they had been staying at the house.

"It's not a problem, dear," Loren said. "We've planned on staying at my house to get things packed and sorted, what we plan on keeping and taking to your mother's and what we're going to get rid of. So you and the boys can stay here for a little while."

"I don't know if we'll keep on staying here. I just felt that we needed to get out of the house for the immediate future. I don't know what's going on with Brandon but hopefully this will pass and he will leave us alone. So, are you going to live in Mom's house? What are you going to do with your house?" Amy asked.

"We figured we'd stay here because of the proximity to you and the boys. Actually, I like it a little better because of the shed in the back. I can use it for a work shed. I was going to put one at my house but the back yard is not as large as your mother's. And is has so many trees I'd have to have someone come in and cut a few down to make room. No, this is a better idea. And I have a friend that is going to rent my house for a while. He's out of the country right now but will be back in a couple of weeks. He and his wife are adopting a child from China and they're staying there until all the paperwork is completed. They were in the process of building a house when they found out a child was available so they'll need a place to stay until it's completed. We'll see what happens after that."

"A baby from China? That sounds so wonderful. I hope I can meet them. Well, the boys and I have to get back to our lives. It's good to see you returned safe and sound and didn't end up at the bottom of the ocean."

"What a silly thought," Sarah said. "The cruise was wonderful, you should take one if you ever get an opportunity. Or make an opportunity to go. You'd love it."

Amy and the boys went back to their house and it appeared just as they had left it. Any wasn't sure what she expected. She didn't think Brandon would vandalize their house but she apparently thought he'd do something with the uneasy feeling she had all weekend. Now that her mother was back, their routine could go back to normal. She felt she needed to have another talk with Sean and then one with the counselor at school.

"Sean, I want to talk to you about something. I don't want to scare you but I want you to be aware. When I'm at work, I want you to stay close to Gram. I don't think you should be out riding your bike for a while."

"Why? Do you think something's going to happen to me? Is Dad going to get rid of me? He said he would. Why would he do that? Why doesn't he like me?"

Amy could see he was getting upset. "I don't know that he would do any thing to you. I don't think he said what he did because he doesn't like you. I think it was because he uses drugs and they make him do things he wouldn't ordinarily do. When a person uses drugs they don't think right and they don't behave right. But just to be safe, I want you to stay in the house after school and let Gram answer the phone. Okay? And if anything happens you can call me and let me know. I taught you how to call 911 if there is an emergency. If something happens, though I don't think anything will, but if it does call 911 and they'll help you. Really, I think everything is going to be okay."

He looked a little more reassured. Amy helped him to get his clothes ready for school the next day then the three of them sat down and played some games to get their mind off Brandon's threats. The next day Amy called the school counselor.

"Mrs. Whitten, I felt like I should call and let you know what happened last week. Sean's father called several times, most likely high on drugs. He made, well, not really threats but comments that were very upsetting. He was desperate for money and said we were the reason he didn't have any. He said he should get rid of us. That was the comment he made to Sean. Unfortunately, Sean answered the phone while I was at work and had to deal with his father's desperation. He's pretty scared and while I hope it was just Brandon spouting off, I don't want him showing up at school and frightening Sean worse. I just wanted to let you know just in case something happens or Sean acts out again."

"This is so sad. Sean has been doing much better lately. He's pretty insecure and this won't help. He has a session with me today. I'm glad you told me what was going on.

I'll see what he has to say about it. He has been opening up a little with me. I know he feels rejected by his father and although it was a bad situation, rejection to a child is hard to deal with. This just intensifies the feeling, if he thinks his father wants to get rid of him. Mrs. Alexander, have you spoken with the police?" the counselor asked.

"Yes, I called them Friday night after I got his last call."

"Good. It may be nothing but better safe than sorry. Thanks again for calling."

She was glad she called. It was good to know that Sean was doing better in school. She hoped this would not be a big set back. Business was back to usual and the rest of Amy's week flew by. Evenings were spent wondering what Marshall and Alyssa had to talk about for hours on end. Occasionally when he got off the phone he'd tell her she had gotten a call. She'd have to return the call most likely hours after she'd received one. Often it was Lydia calling to check up on her. She had grown to cherish her friendship with Lydia.

"Sorry to be returning your call so late," she said one evening after a prolonged conference between Marshall and his phone companion.

"Are you just now getting phone privileges?" Lydia asked with a giggle.

"Yes. One day you will have a teenager and won't be allowed to use your own phone. You'll see how it is," Amy told her.

"Well, as long as it is with someone like Marshall, I don't care. Carlie will have a strict mother but if she chooses well, it will be easier on her. I called to see what you had planned for Marshall's birthday next week. If you don't have anything planned I thought perhaps you can have a few people to come to the restaurant for a nice dinner. We're starting a new feature, musical entertainment. Next weekend a young performer will be singing here and it would be good to get a review from the younger audience. What do you think?"

"Sounds good to me but I'll have to ask the young man in question. I know what ever we do will include Alyssa. This way it can include the families as well. I'll let you know."

"Okay. And while we are on the subject of Marshall I was wondering if he would like a part time job. He was great last week. It wouldn't be a whole lot of hours because I know he is involved with school but enough to earn a little money of his own and help me out at the same time."

"I'll ask him. He said he enjoyed it. And if he's starting to date, he can spend his own money. I like that idea. Thanks Lydia."

"No problem. Let me know about the party and tell him to call me about the job. Talk to you later."

Amy did not want to think about her baby dating but she supposed she should be realistic, he was about to turn sixteen and he would be dating. She would have to go get him a gift the next day. She had put it off because she didn't know what to get him. She had finally settled on getting him the computer program he had been asking for. It would be a little expensive for her, especially since she was no longer getting any child support. She had discussed it with her boss and he had agreed to let her do some additional work at the office and give her a raise. It would actually benefit them both in the long run.

The next morning Amy sent Sean and Marshall to their grandparents to help clean out their garage and the shed for Loren to began moving his things in. She headed for the mall. After parking and noting where she parked she headed for the computer store. She had forgotten in the past where she had parked and walked the whole parking lot to find her car. Once inside she decided to do some browsing and enjoy herself. She stopped in and purchased the gift then went and bought a nice card and gift wrap. She wished he was still a little boy and impishly picked out a toy just for the fun of it. After a bit she decided a drink and a snack was in order and headed for the food court. As she was standing in line she noticed a young girl looking like her world was falling apart. She was crying and looked absolutely in agony. Amy left her spot to see if she was alright. As she got nearer she realized it was Lacy.

"Lacy, are you alright?" she asked.

Lacy's eyes, brimming with tears looked shocked to see her. It would be impossible for her to deny there was a problem. And she didn't even try. She began to cry all the harder. Amy sat down next to her and put her arm around her. She didn't pull away, instead she leaned into her and sobbed.

"It wasn't supposed to be like this. Nothing is turning out right. I don't know what to do," Lacy said.

"What's wrong? Is there anything I can do to help?" Amy asked.

"Nobody can help me. Everything is a mess."

"Can you tell me what's wrong?"

Lacy sat up and looked at Amy. "Can't you tell? I'm pregnant."

Amy looked at the girl. She had worn baggy clothing every time she had seen her so it was hard to tell anything. But this time it was obvious that Lacy had gained some weight, a lot of weight, around her middle.

"How far along are you?"

"Seven months. I can't hide it any more. Though I don't really have to at home. Mom is about as aware as the Pope. She has a new boyfriend and he is all she pays attention to. I've been watching Stevie while she runs around like a kid. It makes me sick. My boyfriend said he loved me and one day we'd be together. But he lied to me. He already has a family and told me to deal with it by myself. But I don't know what to do," she said as she began crying again.

"Have you seen a doctor?" Amy asked.

"No. I don't have any money."

Amy realized Lacy needed direction. "What do you think will happen when you tell your mother? Do you think she'll help you?

"No. She told me if I ever got pregnant I was on my own. She won't help me."

"I'll do what I can to help you. But first we have to talk to your mother since you're a minor. We'll go from there. Let's go talk to her."

Amy lead Lacy out of the mall to her car. She was surprised that Lacy was seven months along and her mother had not noticed. It was very obvious the girl was heavy with child.

"I knew you were different when I met you that night at your son's party. Your kinder than my mom. You have something in your eyes that shows you are a good person. I want to keep my baby, even if I have to do it alone. But I want to be a good mother, to raise my child to be a better person than I am. Do you think that I can go to church or am I too bad since I'm pregnant and not married?

"Lacy, you can certainly go to church. God loves you no matter if you are pregnant. He doesn't see you as too bad to love. He sees you as his child and is rejoicing that you want to have a relationship with him and are willing to raise your child to know him."

"He sees me as his child? Like he's my father?"

"Absolutely. You are his little girl and he loves you very much. He says we are the apple of his eye."

Lacy began crying again but her face registered joy instead of sorrow. Amy could not help but shed a tear of her own as they drove to Lacy's house.

Chapter Eleven

As Amy stood at the front door of Lacy's house, she felt somewhat silly. Lacy stood there with her even though it was her home. She wondered why the girl didn't just walk in and invite her to come with her. Karen opened the door and looked as if she wondered the same thing.

"Lacy, why are you ringing the door bell?" Karen asked her daughter. "Amy, come in. I'm on the phone but have a seat."

Amy followed Lacy into the living room. They sat on the sofa as Karen finished her phone conversation.

"I'm back, it was only Lacy," she said, picking up the phone. "That sounds wonderful. I am so looking forward to the weekend. I have my bags packed and made arrangements for Stevie to stay with a friend so I'm ready to go. And I'll see you tomorrow night. I love you too. Bye."

Karen hung the phone up and turned to Amy.

"I have the most wonderful boyfriend. We're taking a weekend trip, just the two of us, and staying in the mountains. I'm really looking forward to the trip. I'm surprised to see you. What can I do for you?" she asked.

Amy just looked at her for a moment. Several thoughts crossed her mind. She could not have been dating this man for more than a couple of months at the very most and yet she told him she loved him and was planning a trip out of town with him. And Lacy was sitting in the same room with her and she had not even noticed her condition. No wonder Lacy said she hadn't had to hide it from her mother, she was oblivious to her own daughter's needs.

"Um, I ran into Lacy at the mall," Amy said, pointing to Lacy. "She was very upset and I told her I would come and talk to you with her."

"Why does she need you to talk to me? I'm her mother, she can talk to me without someone helping her."

"I can talk to you all day long but you don't hear me," Lacy said. "All you think about and the only person you pay any attention to is your precious Neal. You haven't even paid any attention to Stevie, you just ship him off to someone's house and run after Neal like you were a teenager. You're worse than me and it makes me sick watching you."

"Lacy, you need to watch your mouth. I take care of Stevie. There is nothing wrong with me falling in love and wanting to spend time with my boyfriend."

"You don't take care of Stevie, I do. I have done his laundry, fed him dinner, made him take a bath and do his homework. I have cleaned the house and lied to the bill collectors because you haven't paid the bills. All you have done is chase after a man who would rather chase after me. I've seen the looks he gives me and it gives me the creeps. And you're too blind to see the truth. How can you say you are in love with this man you've only known for six weeks?" Lacy threw back at her mother.

"How dare you talk to me like that? You're just jealous that I have a boyfriend."

Amy listened to the conversation and thought it sounded like two teenagers instead of a mother and her daughter. She wondered if this was a typical conversation between the two. If it was, no wonder Lacy was in the predicament she was.

"That's just how blind you are," Lacy screamed at her mother. "Look at me. Do I look like I'm jealous about a boyfriend? I'm seven months pregnant. The last thing I am is jealous."

Lacy stood up and pulled her baggy shirt tight against her belly and Karen looked shocked at the sight.

"You never pay any attention to me. You are always focused on the latest man in your life. And there have been plenty. I have had to fight off their hands and hide from their lecherous looks. But you didn't even notice that," Lacy finished in tears.

"Whose baby are you carrying?" Karen asked in anger.

"Don't worry. It's not any of your boyfriends that got me pregnant."

"Well, someone did. Who was it?"

Lacy turned away, refusing to answer the question.

"Don't answer me then. But what do you plan to do with it?"

"What do I plan to do with it, you mean my baby? I'm going to keep it."

"Think again, little lady. I'm not going to raise it. If you keep it you will have to do it somewhere else."

"So your kicking me out. Where am I supposed to go?"

"That's not my problem. Call your dad. Maybe he'll feel sorry for you and take you in."

Lacy looked at her mother, hurt filling her eyes. She took the phone and went to the other room to make the call.

"How did you get involved in this?" Karen asked Amy.

"I saw her crying at the mall. I asked her what was wrong and it kind of just poured out. She said you probably wouldn't take it well. Are you really going to make her leave? She really needs your help right now."

"I'm not going to raise her child. I want to have my own life. I'm not starting over raising her baby. She got herself in this mess and she will have to find her own way out of it. It's not my problem."

Lacy came back in the room.

"Dad's out of town. Kim said she'd have him call when he got back. I told her I didn't know where I would be so I'd call him later. Can I stay here until he gets back?"

"No you cannot. I'll not have Stevie having to look at you and ask questions."

"He's going to ask questions if I'm not here. Who's going to take care of him, do all the things I've been doing?"

"I'm fully capable of taking care of my son. Gather your things. When you get in touch with your dad, he can bring you back for what you can't take now."

Amy supposed the visit was over. She waited for Lacy to gather a few things. She wondered what to do with the girl. She couldn't really take her into her own home. She had to think about her own sons. But then she couldn't really turn her out on the side of the road. When she got home she'd call her mother. Perhaps she had an idea where a homeless, unwed mother-to-be could stay. As she and Lacy got in the car, she saw Lacy had a hopeless expression on her face. The girl probably wasn't more than fifteen years old. She was terribly young to have such a burden to carry, especially alone.

"Lacy, what about the baby's father? Are you sure he doesn't want to help you?"

"I'm sure. He told me that he wanted to be with me until I told him I was pregnant. He told me to get rid of it. I hate to hear people talk like that. It's not like it's a bag of trash you can just take out. It's a baby, my baby. I know I'm young but I'm not dumb. I can take care of a baby. My baby will love me even if I mess up and I will love her even if she makes a mistake. That's what's important, to love them no matter what. I asked him if he would marry me. He told me that he couldn't and even if he could, he wouldn't. He said he had a wife and child and didn't need another one. I asked him if he had a wife and child what was he doing with me. He said 'having fun.' I haven't seen him in four months. I've been trying to figure out what to do. I knew my mom wouldn't help me. I just don't know what to do," she sobbed.

"We'll figure it out," Amy told her, patting her hand though she herself had no idea of how to help. She wondered how old the man was who had gotten Lacy pregnant and if there should be some concern about that. They pulled into the driveway and Amy wondered what to tell the boys. Marshall would be okay but she worried about Sean's reaction. Even after all they had been through, he was very naïve about some things. Marshall was in the kitchen when they walked in. He eyed Lacy but said nothing. She was obviously expecting him to make some comment and looked prepared to defend herself.

"Lacy, would you like something to eat or drink?" Amy asked her.

"Maybe some water," she replied.

Marshall got a glass and poured her some cold water from the refrigerator and handed it to her. As she drank the water she watched Marshall for a reaction. He took some cheese and sliced it into squares and got some crackers and put them on a plate. He handed the plate to her and asked her if she had heard about the exchange student at school. He lead her into the living room and talked to her as if this was an ordinary event. Amy watched her son put their guest at ease and marveled at his wisdom. She went to call her mother as the kids talked about school.

"Mom, I need some advice. I know of a young girl that is in the family way and needs a place to stay for a short while. Do you know of a place?" Amy asked her mother.

"No, not right off the top of my head. I'm sure there's places in town but I don't know where. May I ask who the girl is?"

"Well, I'm sure you'll hear sooner or later. Remember Sean's friend Stevie? It's his sister Lacy."

"No. That girl's only a child."

"I know. Her mother told her she couldn't stay in the house. She tried to call her father but he's out of town. I'd let her stay here but I don't know where I'd put her."

"Do you think she'd mind staying here?"

"Mom, you can't take her in. You just got married."

"Well, it's not like it's going to be forever. Loren and I will love to have her as a guest. I remember her from the party, she needs someone to care about her, to show her Christ's love. And she can help me sort through all this stuff. It'll be fine, if she doesn't mind staying with us old folks."

"I'll ask her. If she's comfortable with it, I'll bring her down. Thanks."

Amy hung up the phone and listened to the kids laugh. She was pleased that Marshall hadn't judged Lacy and was treating her kindly. She hoped that this would end well for both Lacy and her baby.

"Well, I have a question for Lacy," Amy said entering the room. She noticed Lacy looked relaxed and happier. "If you don't mind, I have found you a temporary place to stay until you can talk to your dad. My mother said she would love for you to stay with her. She just got married and she and her husband are sorting through their things to see what they want to keep and what they want to discard. She said if you were willing you could stay there and help them in the process."

"Really? They'd take in a stranger? I mean, I think that's very kind, and no, I wouldn't mind but they'd really take me in? Your mother just got married? That's so cool, you know, that older people still fall in love and get married."

Amy agreed inwardly. Love was a special thing and she was glad it was not just for the young. She took Lacy's hand and guided her toward the car. Yep, God was still in control.

Chapter Twelve

Amy was dealing with an upset customer on Tuesday afternoon. The woman just did not want to understand what Amy was trying to tell her.

"Mrs. Moseby, I discussed with you the problem with your vehicle. Remember? I told you that it needed a lot of work and it would be expensive. We discussed doing your repairs in stages, doing the most critical things first. Until all the work is done, it's not going to run at its best. It will still make some noise and use a lot of gas. You said you could only afford these repairs at this time. We've still got a couple of repairs to make but it is safe for you to drive."

"I know what we discussed but I don't understand why it's still making that noise."

"Because we didn't work on that noise. I know it's irritating but it's not critical. We needed to get your car where it was safe for you to drive, where it won't break down and leave you stranded. The next time you bring it in, we'll work on that noise. We just want you to be safe until you can bring it in for the rest of your repairs."

"When can I bring it back? That noise grates on my nerves."

"You can bring it back as soon as you have the money. It's up to you. We'll do it when ever you want."

"When ever I want? Well, as soon as I get another check I want that noise fixed."

"That's fine. Do you want to set up an appointment now or call me later?"

"I'll call you later for the appointment. Thank you for your time."

"Thank you for coming in and letting me explain the situation. Call me when your ready for the next repair."

Amy had explained the situation to her customer three times now. Hopefully she understood it now. Amy did not understand why people got so upset over noises when they weren't as big a problem as a car that wouldn't run right. But they would come in complaining about a noise when the car sputtered and chugged like it was in the throes of death. They were less interested in getting their car in good running shape than in getting rid of an irritating noise.

Turning to answer the phone, she thought about those irritating noises and wishing this was one she could quiet.

"Hello. Caseman's Auto Repair," she said into the phone.

"Amy, Sean didn't get off the bus today," Sarah said anxiously on the other end.

"What do you mean he didn't get off the bus?" Amy responded, suddenly alarmed.

"He didn't get off the bus. I was in the yard talking to Phyllis next door and her daughter got off but Sean didn't. I asked her where Sean was and she said he wasn't on the bus. She said some woman came and got him before he got on the bus. I thought if it had been you, you'd have called and let me know."

"Yes I would. Have you called the school?"

"No, I called you immediately. You'd know who to talk to."

"Okay. I'll call them now."

Hanging up and dialing the school's number, Amy had no idea who would be picking her son up. He knew not to leave with strangers.

"Price Elementary," a voice answered.

"Hello. This is Amy Alexander, Sean Alexander's mother. Sean did not get on the bus today to come home. One of the other students said a woman came and got him just before he got on the bus. I don't know who that may have been but they did not have my permission to pick him up."

"What bus does he ride? I'll find the teacher that loads those students and see what happened."

"It's bus 122."

"Okay. Hold on."

Amy waited what seemed like hours before the woman came back. "Mrs. Bailey said the woman came up and told her Sean's mother was in an accident. She said the woman looked panicked and she grabbed Sean and pulled him away. Mrs. Bailey told her she couldn't take him without permission from his mother. The woman said his mother was in the hospital and couldn't give permission. Sean was very upset and pulled away and went with the woman. He was crying and saying he needed to get to you."

"Did Mrs. Bailey give you a description of the woman?"

"Here's Mrs. Bailey. She finished her duties and can talk now."

"Mrs. Alexander. I'm sorry. I tried to keep him from leaving with the woman but she was insistent. I didn't know what to do. Sean went willingly with her so I thought he knew her."

"What did she look like?"

"She had big red hair, you know, lots of wild curls. She was dressed in a fancy pants suit and wore lots of makeup. Do you have any idea who it was?"

"I'm afraid so. Did she ask for him by name?"

"Yes she did. Who was it? Is he in danger?"

"I don't know but there is that possibility. It's his father's girlfriend. I don't know her but I know this is not good. I need to call the police. Thank you for your help," Amy said hanging up the phone.

She dialed 911 and tried to keep calm while reporting her son's abduction.

"911. What's your emergency?"

"My son has been taken. He's seven years old. A woman took him from school a short while ago when he was getting on the bus to come home. Based on the description of the woman, it's my ex-husband's girlfriend. I don't know where she lives."

"About how long ago did this happen?"

"I found out about five minutes ago when my mother called to let me know he didn't get off the bus. He gets out of school at three o-five. I guess it's been about forty-five minutes since she took him."

"Do you recall what he was wearing?"

Amy described Sean and the woman who had picked him up. She told the operator that the woman had told the teacher and Sean that she was in the hospital, which was why Sean had gone with the woman although he had been instructed not to do that. Unfortunately, she did not have any idea where Brandon and the woman lived.

"You said you don't know where your ex-husband lives. Any idea where she may have taken him?"

"Not a clue. His father is abusive, at least he was to me. He has an anger issue. I'm afraid he'll hurt my son to hurt me. He has been calling asking for money. He's deep into drugs."

Amy gave her information on Brandon and told her about the threatening phone calls.

"We'll put out an alert for your son and the woman," the operator told Amy before disconnecting.

When she finished the call, she called her mother back.

"I called the school and found out it was Brandon's girlfriend that took Sean," she told Sarah

"Why would she do that?" Sarah asked.

"I don't know. I talked to the police and they're putting out a child alert on Sean. I'm going to head for home."

"Should you do that? I mean where would Brandon call you at this time of day?"

"Who knows? He's been calling the house though I don't know why. He knows where I work."

"Okay. If he calls before you get home I'll call you on your cell phone."

Amy told her boss what was going on. She apologized about all the problems and her being away from her job. He said he understood. Since it was Tuesday, it wouldn't be a problem. She hoped the problem would be solved long before the difficult end of the week. She headed home not knowing if hearing from Brandon would be good or bad.

"God, please protect Sean. Don't let Brandon hurt him. Keep him in your care, send your angels to protect him. Please don't let anything happen to him."

Amy prayed all the way home, her cell phone never ringing. She ran into the house and found Sarah and Marshall huddled by the phone. Marshall looked angry.

"You've not heard from him yet?" Amy asked.

"No. I can't believe he'd do something like this. Why would he hurt his own son? What is going on in his mind?" Sarah asked, nearly in tears.

"Nothing is going on in his mind. His mind is wasted on drugs. He's never thought of me and Sean as his sons. We were just in his way. He'd better not hurt Sean," Marshall said angrily.

"We don't know he plans to hurt Sean. He could just be trying to get money from me. At least I hope that's all it is. But I don't have any money to give him unless he wants the last five dollars I have," Amy said pacing the room.

The phone didn't ring even with all three of the wishing it would. Not even a telemarketer called. Amy was nearly at her wits end. Loren had joined them and Amy had called the police to see if there was an update. They told her there wasn't and to try to stay off the phone should Brandon call. He finally called at nearly eight thirty that evening.

Amy snatched the phone up on the first ring.

"Hello," she answered breathlessly.

"Amy," Brandon said.

"Where's my son?" she yelled into the phone.

"He's okay. Calm down."

"Calm down? You steal my son and then tell me to calm down? I want my son!"

"You can have him. And I didn't steal him," Brandon whispered.

"No, your girlfriend kidnapped him. Is she doing all your dirty work now?"

"Look. It wasn't my idea. I didn't know she was going to take him from school. I told her not to do it and she did it anyway. She wanted me to hold him until you came up with some money. I don't want to involve the kids in our fight. Despite what you may think, I wouldn't hurt them. But I do need some money."

"I've told you, I don't have any money. You've threatened to make them disappear. Why would I think you wouldn't hurt them?"

"They're my kids too. What do you think I am, some kind of a monster. I only said that to scare you."

"You've hurt me enough to think of you as a monster. And you have my son. He's probably scared to death. He already thinks you're going to hurt him."

"Why would he think that, because that's what you told him?"

"Because that's what you told him. And he is aware that you have no qualms about hitting us for no reason."

"I never hit him for no reason. I punished him for breaking the rules or making a mess. He had to learn to behave. All you ever did was coddle him. I had to teach him about real life."

"Does real life include beating up his wife and getting hooked on drugs?"

"I'm not going to fight with you over this. Just give me a hundred dollars, okay."

"So you're holding Sean ransom for a hundred dollars? Well, I don't have a hundred dollars. "

"No, I'm not holding him ransom. I don't want him here. I just want some money. I'll call you in a little while," Brandon said, hanging up the phone.

"Brandon, don't hang up on me. Where is my son?" Amy yelled, though the line was dead.

She collapsed on the sofa weeping.

"What did he say?" Sarah asked.

"He said he had Sean. He asked for a hundred dollars. He said it wasn't his idea to get Sean, it was his girlfriend's. She wanted him to hold him until I gave him some money. I just don't have a hundred dollars."

"I'll give you a hundred dollars," Loren said.

"If I give in to him, he'll be calling every week for money, pulling another stupid stunt."

"But what about Sean?" he asked.

"I don't know. He said he'd call back in a little while."

Brandon called back about twenty minutes later.

"He's at the store by the bank. I dropped him off and told him to stay there. I told him you'd come get him. I wasn't trying to kidnap him," he said.

The line went dead as soon as he told Amy where she could find her son.

"He's dropped Sean off at the store by the bank. I'm going to get him," she said slamming the phone down and grabbing her car keys.

Marshall was on her heels as she ran out of the house. She drove to the store and found Sean standing by the coolers in the back. He looked relieved to see his mother. They climbed into the car, squeezing Sean in the middle.

"You okay, little brother?" Marshall asked him, ruffling his hair.

"I'm okay. Dad and that woman was yelling at each other. He said he told her not to get me from school because it would get him in trouble. I'm sorry Mom that I went with her. She said you was hurt and in the hospital. I was afraid I wouldn't see you again. I'm sorry," he said as he began to sob.

"It's okay, I understand. We've just got to be real careful now. Did your dad hurt you or anything?" she said.

"No. They got in a big fight and he hit her and she went to the bedroom. He grabbed me and pushed me out the door to the car. He didn't even say anything to me until we got to the store. He said to wait by the back until you got there. Mom, I don't think I like Dad. Will God be mad at me if I don't like Dad?"

"I think God understands," she told him.

When they arrived back at the house Amy wasn't sure who was more upset, her mother or step-father. They made over him like he'd returned from a war.

"Do I have to go to school tomorrow?" he asked.

"Yes, you do. But I'm going to talk to the school and make sure this doesn't happen again," Amy told her son.

She hoped there'd be no repeat episode. She finally ushered her parents out the door and the boys to bed. Sean was still unsettled and asked to sleep in her bed. She thought under the circumstances it would be a good idea. He got into his pajamas and crawled into her bed and was asleep within a few minutes. Amy sat in the living room for little while. As she was getting ready for bed, the phone rang.

"Hello," she answered quietly.

"I could have gotten rid of him. I could have taken him somewhere you'd never find him," Brandon said, his voice indicating that he was on something.

Amy shut her bedroom door where Sean lay sleeping.

"How can you say that? Have you no feelings for your children? Do you realize what a mistake that would have been? You would have been the first suspect the police would have come after."

"The mistake was letting you have those kids. I never wanted any kids. I wanted it to be just you and me. Things would have been different without them. Then you got all mixed up in church and religion. God doesn't care about you. You are nothing to him."

"I have always been in church, even when we were dating. I didn't change, you did. And God does care about me. He loves me and I mean everything to him. He has done to much for me, taken care of me too many times for me to believe he doesn't love me."

"Amy, you're sick in the head. What would God want from you?"

"He doesn't want something from me. He wants me. He wants me to love him, to have a personal relationship with him as his child."

"That's so lame. He hates us all. We're all screw-ups. I don't blame him for hating us. It's what we deserve."

Brandon's voice was getting weaker and more slurred. Amy was straining to hear what he was saying and the line went dead. As she sat holding the phone, she thought about occasions God showed his love to her. She knew she was loved by her Heavenly Father. She had peace in her heart about that and she embraced the feeling.

Chapter Thirteen

Marshall fussed over his appearance like a girl, Amy thought as she watched him get ready for his birthday dinner. He had been pleased with the idea of a nice dinner and it had fit in with her previous plans. It had started out small but had grown to include more than Amy had anticipated. Of course Alyssa and her parents were coming but as other family members heard about the evening they wanted to be included. The list now included Sarah, Loren, Lacy, Sean, Dillon, Craig and his girlfriend Melody. Sarah had insisted that Lacy be included and Marshall had agreed. No reason to make her feel worse than she already did by excluding her.

Amy had to admit that Lacy seemed to be blooming under her mother's care. She had tried to call her father again but he was not due to return home for a couple more weeks. Lacy's step-mother Kim seemed to be a kind woman and understanding of Lacy's plight. She said she didn't think it would be a problem as long as Lacy obeyed the house rules but she couldn't make the decision for her husband. He said he wanted to talk to Lacy before she moved in. Lacy was fine with that, she had said.

"Does this tie go with this shirt?" Marshall asked his mother.

"Yes, it does. But you do know that you don't have to wear a tie, don't you?" she answered.

"I know. I just want to look good. It's a special occasion and I want it to feel special. I don't mean just because it's my birthday celebration but because everyone is getting together. That's what makes it special. The people I love most are going to be together and I want to show them what they mean to me."

"Lacy and Craig and Melody is going to be there. Do you love them too," Sean said teasingly.

"Yes I do. Sean, you know that God has commanded us to love everyone. Lacy and Craig and Melody are my friends and I love them. Not in the same way I love you and Mom. They're people that mean a lot to me and God loves them so I love them."

Sean looked at Marshall with a bit of awe. "You even love Lacy? Her momma don't."

"Well, that's her momma's problem. She doesn't know God. If she did she would love and forgive Lacy for making a mistake. God has already forgiven her so we can't not forgive her. Right?"

"I guess so. God forgives us even if our parents don't?"

"That's right. God forgives us even if nobody else in the world does. We just have to ask to be forgiven of our mistakes, our sins, and if we really mean it, he does. People don't always forgive others because they don't want to let go of the hurt they feel. But if we obey God, we have to forgive others just like we want to be forgiven. You want to be forgiven don't you?"

"Yes."

"Then you have to forgive others. Remember when Jesus was hanging on the cross and he prayed for God to forgive those men that hung him? That would be the hardest thing to do, to forgive someone who was killing your or

99

killed someone you loved. But if Jesus did it, he expects us to do it. And just because Lacy made a mistake and got pregnant before she got married, that's not a reason at all to not forgive her."

Amy listened to the conversation between her sons. She had no idea that the situation with Lacy would be a learning experience for all of them. God really did work in mysterious ways, she thought. As they drove to the restaurant, Amy asked Marshall whether he had talked to Lydia about the job.

"Yes ma'am. She told me I could work four days a week. Weekdays would only be about four hours and I could work a full shift on Saturdays. I can get off the bus after school at the restaurant but you'll have to pick me up after work until I can get a car. I'm going to save my money to buy a car. Loren said he'd help me pick one out."

"That's a good idea. But I don't want you to work so much your grades drop. Be sure to not overburden yourself and let it effect your grades."

"I won't. I want to go to college. I'm glad you care. You know, you really are a great mom. If I could have chose any mother I wanted, I would choose you."

"Yeah, you're the best mom in the world," Sean echoed.

Amy was having a hard time driving. Her eyes had tears and she could hardly see the road. She had not thought to get such praise from her children. She would have to pass the praise to her mother. She deserved to be told that she was the best mom in the world too. When they pulled into the parking lot, Amy saw Alyssa was just as dressed up as Marshall. Perhaps this would be their first official date. They went in and Lydia showed them to a section near the rear of the restaurant. A piano had been set up nearby. Amy remembered going to a restaurant that boasted musical entertainment when she and Brandon were dating. It gave the restaurant a nice atmosphere. She thought the addition to the restaurant would be good.

Lacy looked very pretty. She was wearing a pink maternity outfit and had her hair pulled back. Amy did not realize what an attractive girl she was until she saw her in something besides baggy black clothes. She had finally seen a doctor and it was determined that she was having a boy. Lacy was trilled. Sarah had talked to the ladies at church and they were planning a baby shower for Lacy. Alyssa had decided that she would help out and had even taken over. She wanted to make it very personal for Lacy and for the younger girls to be involved.

Dillon was showing some interest in Lacy during the dinner, though Amy was not exactly sure why. He asked her if she had a name for her baby.

"My dad's name is James so I'm thinking maybe Dustin James. I don't know for sure though. Sometimes I like it and sometimes I don't know," she said.

"It's a nice name. You could call him D.J." Dillon suggested.

"Right. Just like you were called when you were little," Evelyn teased her son.

"That's not what I meant. I had even forgotten you called me that," he laughed.

They all had a good time and after the table was cleared, every one put a small gift on the table.

"I thought the dinner was my gift. It was all I expected," Marshall said as he began opening gifts. He thanked everyone for their thoughtfulness.

Amy was glad that everyone had come to dinner. It would be a treasured memory for both her and Marshall. As they were all prepared to get up from the table, Loren said there was one more small gift he wanted to present to Marshall. He handed him a small box. Marshall opened the gift and looked confused. It was a key chain.

"It's really nice," he told his new grandfather.

"Do you really like it? I looked for just the right one. It'll look real good with this key on it, don't you think?" Loren asked handing him a key.

Marshall took the key and looked at it like it was the strangest thing he had ever seen. Amy held her breath. She was not sure she was ready for what was to come.

"It's a key," Loren said. "You've seen one before haven't you."

"Yes sir," Marshall replied.

"Well, it's your key. Enjoy it."

"Yes sir," Marshall said again, totally confused.

Loren patted him on the back and laughed. "It fits the ignition of the car at the house. Want to come look at it?"

"Sure," Marshall replied, with big expressive eyes.

The whole party drove to Sarah's house to see the car. Marshall was speechless. He just stood there and stared. Amy was pretty speechless herself. It was the last thing she expected. She caught her mother's eye and questioned her silently. Sarah just smiled and winked in return. Loren came and stood by her side and watched as Marshall finally opened the door and sat in the car. He leaned over and unlocked the other door and Sean and Alyssa climbed in.

"I know you think this is an expensive gift for someone new to the family. But I remember being a boy much like Marshall. My dad passed away and my mother was left to care for me and my brothers and sisters. She really struggled. I watched her try to provide for us and do what was best for us with very little to work with. I have a great respect for single mothers. It was the kindness of someone outside our family that made the difference for us. A gentleman would leave food on our porch or a bolt of cloth for dresses for my sisters. He wouldn't do it where my mother could see him, she was pretty proud but she recognized the compassion of the giver.

"He gave me my first car and I was able to get a job and help my mother. That to me was the greatest gift, to be able to contribute to my family's needs. It wasn't a great car but it ran for a long time, until I was able to get something better. I made a silent promise to that man that I would do the same for someone in the same situation. You think Marshall is the receiver of a great gift, but really it is me that got the better gift. God blessed me and gave me the ability to bless others. That's one of the reasons Sarah and I took Lacy in. To bless her as we have been blessed. One day I hope Marshall can pass that blessing on to someone else. That's how blessings work best, passed from one to another," Loren said as he put his arm around Amy.

Amy couldn't hold back her tears. She looked up at her step-father. She couldn't express the feeling that she was the most blessed without completely breaking down in tears. But Loren saw it her eyes and hugged her a little tighter.

"You know he'll want to go get his license as soon as possible," he said.

"Yeah, Monday will take forever getting here. I guess I'll have to take off from work early to take him up there for his test."

"I can take him. I remember taking my oldest son to take his test. I wasn't sure he was ready for that step. He was but I just didn't want him growing too soon. It turned out to be fun for both of us. I lost him a few years later to an illness and grieved so much for him I forgot I had another son and a daughter. I missed doing those things with them. By the time I got a grip on life again, they were grown. I am making it up by being the best grandpa I can. You don't mind, do you? I don't want to overstep my bounds."

"I don't mind at all. You deserve the opportunity. I'm sure Marshall would love for you to go along with him. Thank you."

"Thank you," Loren said.

The party broke up and everyone began heading for home. Marshall was reluctant to leave the car. Loren told him to come over the next day after church so he could show him some things about the car. He was going to make sure he knew how to change a flat, check the engine fluids and drive it without any problems. Amy had let him drive through the neighborhoods and to church a time or two. She knew Craig's dad had taken both boys driving on several occasions and both had taken driver's education in school. She was like Loren and didn't want her son to grow up too fast.

At church the next morning Amy felt like she was a part of a huge family. Lydia and Carlie had joined them as well as all of Alyssa's family, including Dillon. He had not made coming to church a priority. She wondered again at his attention to Lacy. While it was true that Lacy was a woman in the physical sense, she was still only sixteen years old. Sarah had talked with her at length about the father of the baby and the only thing she had learned was that he was in his twenties and had played on Lacy's desire to be loved by someone, anyone. Amy wanted to ask Dillon why he was interested in Lacy. Surely a nineteen year old young man would be more interested in a girl closer to his age. She couldn't figure it out. After the service Amy and the boys went to Sarah's house for lunch. Marshall and Loren headed to the car as soon as lunch was over. Sean tagged along to be with the "men."

Lacy had her feet propped up. She looked absolutely miserable with her still expanding girth. But her face was radiant.

"Lacy, do you know Dillon?" Amy asked her.

"Not really. I've seen him around. He's a nice guy," she replied before drifting off to sleep.

Later that evening as they were getting ready for church, Amy went to Marshall's room.

"Is there any reason why Dillon would be interested in Lacy?" she asked him.

"None that I know of personally. But I think he knows the baby's father. Alyssa said he had said something abut the guy, that he did her dirty. She said it seemed like he knew the guy by the way he talked about Lacy."

"Do you think he'd tell who it was?"

"I don't know. Do you want me to ask him?"

"Well, he might be more willing to talk to you than me. Do you mind?"

"No, I'll ask him tonight if he's there. If not as soon as I get a chance. Why does it matter anyway? Lacy said he doesn't want anything to do with the baby and she doesn't want to name him. It might be for the best if we just leave it alone."

"You may be right. I'm really just curious about why Dillon shows her so much attention. I guess I'm afraid he may see her as an easy target and I feel protective of her."

"Mom, Dillon is really a nice guy. I don't think he'd try and take advantage of her."

"I hope not. It's just that she's so young for some one of his age to be interested in." Amy returned to her room and finished dressing for church. She thought it odd that Lacy had become important to all of them in such a short amount of time. Her mother had not even checked on her that Amy knew of. Amy felt it would be such a loss if the two never got back together.

Chapter Fourteen

A s Amy came in from work later in the week, she saw a car she did not recognize parked in her driveway. A small twinge of fear caused her to catch her breath. Who could be at her house? Parking her car, she tried to stay calm as she got out of the car. It may be a friend of her mother's, no need to panic she told herself. Amy hoped the day would come that she would not feel she had to be on her guard all the time. Entering the house she heard a man's voice.

"Hello," she said approaching the stranger sitting in her living room.

"Hello. I'm Lacy's father James Selby. It's nice to meet you."

"Oh, Mr. Selby. It's nice to meet you too," Amy replied, vastly relieved.

Lacy had been coming with Sarah each day to sit with Sean after school. Often she found that Lacy had made cookies for Sean during the day. It showed that she was missing her brother a great deal. She also had given him some much needed help with his math homework. Amy was surprised to see that Lacy was actually very smart, much smarter that she had given her credit for being. Amy realized she had thought Lacy was not very bright because of the situation she had gotten herself into.

"Amy, look at what I made for my baby," Lacy said showing her a small embroidered towel. "Sarah showed me how to do the stitches. It's a burp towel for the baby. It's the first thing I've ever made." Lacy's face was radiant with her accomplishment.

"It's lovely. I used to make things for my baby. You find often though that the first things you make you end up saving. So make a lot of things," Amy said as she looked at the towel Lacy had stitched.

"I've been talking to Lacy about her future," James told Amy. "I'm concerned about how she will care for herself and a baby as young as she is."

"Daddy, I know it'll be hard. I want to finish school. I talked to the counselor and she said I could continue going to school until the baby is born. My teachers can send home work for me to do while I'm out so I won't get behind. And as soon as I'm old enough I plan on getting a job. I don't want to have to be dependent on you for everything I need for my baby," Lacy told her father.

"It sounds like you have it all figured out. But have you forgotten that while you're attending school and working that someone has to keep the baby?"

"No Daddy, I haven't forgotten that. I checked and I can get state help for child care. Once I began working I can pay for the additional cost of someone keeping him in the evenings. I know I won't have much money to spend and I know I'll have to make some sacrifices in the beginning. But I also don't want my baby to grow up thinking his mother didn't love him enough to make sacrifices so she gave him away. Dad, I know what it feels like to think my parents didn't love me and I don't want my baby to feel that way. It'll be hard enough for him to know his father didn't want him. I don't want him to think his mother didn't either."

"Lacy, I don't know where you got the idea that your parents didn't love you. I tried to stay close to you but you pulled away, not me. Every time I came to pick you up you refused to see me. And your mother, well, I don't know what's going on with her."

"I know I acted like a baby. I was jealous of you and Kim. And then you had a baby with her. I thought you would like her baby more than Stevie and me. I'm sorry Daddy. Kim is a really sweet woman and I treated her bad but it was because I was jealous. Do you think she'll forgive me?"

"There is nothing to forgive, sweetheart. But we've got a lot of talking to do and a lot of things to figure out. I want you to understand that if you come live with us, there will be rules that you will have to follow and your share of chores to be done. There will be no boys hanging out at the house and you will not be allowed to just run the streets. Do you understand?"

"Yes sir. I don't plan to do either. I promise I will behave and help out around the house. I really just want to be a good mother to my baby. Can Stevie come over sometimes? I miss him."

"Well, you know your mother has a new man in her life. It seems your mother is going to marry him and he doesn't want a ready made family. Karen has asked me to come get Stevie. He's going to be moving in with us. I don't know what is going on in her head but I'm afraid she's setting herself up for a lot of pain down the road. Stevie isn't too keen on the idea but he's agreeable because you'll be there."

Lacy looked surprised by what her father told her. She had a very solemn look on her face.

"Daddy, he's not really a nice man, this guy Mom's going to marry. He's made some ugly comments to me. It'll be better if Stevie is not around him. When are you going to get him?"

"This weekend. Your mother said I could pick up yours and Stevie's things on Friday. We need to get some things settled at the house. I never realized that I'd be providing living space for so many people. We've got to figure out where everybody is going to sleep, especially two babies. Well, let's get going. Thank you Ms. Alexander and Mrs. Kessler for your help and care for Lacy."

"Dad, it's not like I'm not going to see them again. We all go to church together. They are part of my family. I can keep going to church, can't I?"

James looked confused for a moment. "I guess so if it means so much to you. Sure. We can all use a little more family, I guess."

"Stevie and Sean are best friends. Sean is Amy's son. That's how I met them, through Stevie. He can go to church with me and be with Sean. It'll be good for him."

Lacy gave Amy and Sarah a hug. "I expect a call when it's time for the baby to come. I don't care if it's in the middle of the night. You call me," Sarah told Lacy.

After Lacy and her father left, Sarah sat on the couch. "I've gotten attached to that girl. She's a good kid. She just needed for someone to love her. That boy that she got mixed up with acted like he cared for her. That's why she trusted him. It's a shame he treated her like he did. I hope she has learned that not all that glitters is gold."

"Yeah. I wonder why Karen has decided to have Stevie live with his dad. I couldn't just give up my kids. Speaking of kids, where are mine?"

"Sean is with Loren. They're making something in the shed and they won't let me in. It's supposed to be a surprise. I don't have a clue what they're up to. Marshall is at the library. That boy studies more than any kid I've ever seen."

"He's always been like that. His grades are real important to him. I wish I could find a way to get Sean half as interested as Marshall in making good grades. What's for dinner?"

Amy got up to search for something to prepare for dinner. Sarah continued to sit on the couch, apparently deep in thought. Amy decided on French bread pizzas for supper. As she began preparations, Sarah appeared at the door of the kitchen.

"Amy, do you know someone named Sylvia Porter?" Sarah asked.

"I don't think so. Should I?"

"I don't know. A woman called here today and asked for you. She said her name was Sylvia Porter. She acted like you would know who she was but I don't recall ever hearing you use her name."

"Did she say what she wanted?"

"No. When she asked for you I told her you weren't home from work yet. I asked her if she wanted to leave her number for you to call her back but she said she'd call later."

"I don't recognize the name. Maybe it's a parent of one of the boy's classmates. I guess I'll have to wait and see if she calls back."

Marshall came in with Alyssa in tow.

"Hey, Mom. What's for dinner?" he asked.

"French bread pizza. Are you two working on something for school?" Amy asked.

"I'm not but Alyssa is. She has a report due next week. I took her to the library to get some books. I have a debate this Thursday. Remember that team last year that beat us so bad? They're who we're competing against. We've really been working hard so we at least won't get beat so bad. I think we stand a good chance to win but the others don't agree with me."

"I didn't know you had a competition this week. Did you tell me and I forget or did you forget to tell me?"

"I probably forgot to tell you. Can Alyssa stay for dinner?"

"I suppose so, if she likes pizza."

"I don't think I've ever had French bread pizza," Alyssa said.

"Really? We love it. Mom makes great pizza," Marshall assured her.

"If you don't mind, would you go fetch your brother? He's working on something with Granddad in the shed. Your grandmother is not allowed to see what they're doing but I'm sure it'll be okay for you," Amy said.

Marshall nodded at his mother and he and Alyssa headed out the door.

"They're a cute couple. She is such a sweet girl. I hope though that they don't get too serious right now. They still have so much growing up to do," Sarah said.

"I've talked to Marshall about that. He said he knows that a lot may change when they get into college but right now they enjoy being together. He said they weren't planning on getting married or anything like that. He assures me that they are waiting to see where life takes them before they make any commitments to each other. I think they are both pretty mature and are just enjoying each other's company for the time being."

Sarah didn't respond to Amy's comments. She again appeared to be lost in thought. A few minutes later the kids came in. Amy sent Sean to clean up as Marshall set the table. Sarah went home to prepare dinner for her husband. As they gathered around the table, Marshall handed a plate to Alyssa. She took a tentative bite of the pizza.

"This is good. I'll have to tell my mom to get the recipe from you. I'm sure Dad and Dillon will love it," Alyssa said as she stuffed another bite in her mouth.

"Alyssa, can I ask you something? I'm a little curious about Dillon and his interest in Lacy. Do you have any idea why he's so interested in her?" Amy asked.

"Not really. He's said he's proud she has chosen to keep her baby even though it will be hard on her because she's so young. But beyond that I have no idea. Do you want me to ask him for you?"

"No, that's okay. I was just curious."

They finished dinner and Marshall and Alyssa cleared the table so they could do their homework. Sean and Amy settled in the living room to play a game. Amy had made a set of cards with different vocabulary words on them. Sean would make silly sentences with the words. Amy had found that the game was fun for both of them and Sean got a better grasp on the meaning and use of his vocabulary words. After a while, Marshall took Alyssa home and Amy sent Sean to take his bath. As she was preparing her clothes for work, the phone rang. Because of the relaxed atmosphere during and after dinner, she was unprepared for the call.

"Amy, I need some money," Brandon said, his voice harsh over the phone.

"I told you I didn't have any money," she said, shutting her bedroom door.

"You have some jewelry you can sell. I know you do, I bought it for you. Sell it and give me the money."

"I'm not selling my jewelry so you can go buy drugs. I'm not giving you any money, even if I had it. Clean yourself up and get a job."

"Amy, I'm telling you to get me some money. I'm warning you. I took care of you and your kids for years. Now it's time to give it back. Get me some money."

"It's eight o'clock at night. I couldn't even if I wanted to, which I don't. Stop calling here and threatening me or I will call the police," she said as she hung up the phone.

She was shaking as she opened the door to see if either one of the boys had heard the call. Marshall was not back home yet and Sean was still in the tub. She was relived that the call was made while they were both occupied elsewhere.

She had no idea if Brandon would carry through with his threats but she hoped it would not come to being tested.

As she stood at her door, she was shaking and struggled to keep herself calm. She remembered an incident that had occurred the year before. Brandon had come in late and made sure she was awake. He began ranting at her, though she was never sure what his issue was that night. He hit her and sent her reeling across the bed. As she tried to get to her feet he grabbed her by the hair and told her she needed to find someplace else to live. She yelled that this was her home and if anyone needed to leave it was him. He shook her in his rage, still holding her hair, and pulled her through the house.

Brandon opened the door and threw her out, shutting and locking the door behind her. As she stood on her doorstep in her night clothes sobbing, she was unsure of what to do or expect. She thought of waking Marshall and have him let her in but chose not to do that. She was afraid of dragging him into the fight and Brandon hurting him. She was afraid of what might happen to her sons still inside the house sleeping. At least she hoped they were sleeping. She sat on the steps and cried.

After nearly an hour, the door opened and Brandon looked at her with despair in his eyes. He had told her to come back in the house and apologized for what had happened. She came in but after that never fought back nor argued with him again. She had no idea what he was capable of or would have happened if Brandon had not come to his senses that night. And she had no idea what was going on in his head now. She had learned that anything could happen and to be afraid at those times when he was not rational. This felt like one of those times.

Chapter Fifteen

When Marshall came home from the debate competition that Thursday, he was jubilant. His team had won just as he knew they would. Because the competition was after school, he was off for the evening. He got ready to pick Alyssa up so they could go celebrate the win. Amy and Sean went to Sarah's for the evening. Sean and Loren had finished their secret project and it was ready to be unveiled. Loren had declared it would be presented after dessert. Sean squirmed all through dinner, eager to show off his work. He could hardly wait until dessert was over. Once the plates were finally in the dishwasher, he ushered Loren out to the shed. They came back in struggling with a large sheet covered object.

Sean grinned wildly as he made a big production of removing the sheet. As he saw the looks on his mother and grandmother's faces, he began giggling. It was obvious that he was very proud of his work. Looking at the beautiful baby cradle, Amy wondered how much work he had actually done on it.

"It's beautiful," she exclaimed at the same time Sarah did.

They looked over the cradle and Amy thought it was about the best woodwork she had ever seen. The sides had carved spindles that looked to be professionally made.

"This is absolutely beautiful," she said again. "You two made this?"

"Yep," Sean answered smugly.

"I've done woodwork for years. My dad was a woodworker and my granddad before him. My granddad did it by hand. I have a lathe or I couldn't do much more than make toothpicks. But I love working with wood. Sean actually was a lot of help. Sometimes you need an extra hand and his was just right. Couldn't have done it without him," Loren said with a wink.

Sean beamed. Amy was nearly in tears as she realized the importance Loren had given to Sean's help. She was so grateful that Loren had taken pains to include Sean in his work and make him feel good about himself. When she looked at her mother, the same gratefulness was in her eyes as well.

"Well, what are we going to do with this cradle?" Amy asked, though she was sure what the answer was.

"It's for Lacy's baby," Sean said.

"Oh. For Lacy's baby. Well, I think since you and Granddad did such a fine job on the cradle, I think your mom and I should make something nice to go with it," Sarah said.

"Me? You want me to make something nice? I can't make anything." Amy said to her mother.

"Sure you can. We can make a pad to go in the bottom and a little pillow and a blanket. I know you can do it. We can do it together just like Sean and Loren," Sarah said, giving her a wink.

"Oh. Yeah. We can do that. Sure we can do that. When are we going to give her the gifts?" Amy asked.

"I thought you could give it to her at her baby shower. Isn't the church giving her a shower?" Loren asked.

"Yes, they are. But it's just going to be the ladies there. I think it would be nice to give it to her where you can see her receive it," Amy said.

"Well, that would be nice," he said.

"We'll have a get together here and give it to her. Just a small party. That will be fun and a good excuse to get her back over here. I miss having her around. I'll make some plans for it," Sarah said.

Loren carried the cradle to a corner. Sarah looked like she was already making plans. Amy gathered Sean up and they headed for home. Marshall's car was not in the driveway as they walked back home. Amy hoped he would not be out too late, he had school the next day. As she unlocked the door and let Sean in ahead of her, Amy was suddenly pushed inside. The door slammed behind her and she turned to face Brandon. At least it looked like him. His face was unshaved and his hair was dirty and long. His clothes were equally as dirty and ragged. He had lost a great deal of weight. He no longed looked like the neat business man she had last seen. Now he looked like many of the street bums she saw down town. Amy pushed Sean behind her as she confronted Brandon.

"I don't know why you're here but you need to get out. I told you I don't have any money," she said.

Brandon moved toward her and she backed up pushing Sean with her.

"I know you do. I need some money. I've asked you for it and you have refused. I guess I'll have to get it myself," he said as he pushed her aside and headed for her bedroom.

"Stay out of my room! Get out of my house!" she yelled as he grabbed her jewelry box off her dresser.

Amy didn't have much jewelry but she didn't want to lose what she had. She grabbed for the box to take it out of his hands. Intent of getting the box she didn't see the punch that sent her to the floor. Falling, she hit her head on the bed frame. It was the last thing she felt before she lost consciousness. It was also the moment Marshall entered the fray. Having come in while his mother was struggling with his father, he rushed in the room just as his mother crumpled on the floor.

He snatched the box from his father. Brandon stood staring at Amy's still form for a few moments. He looked at his son and realized Marshall was holding the jewelry box instead of himself. He reached for the box and Marshall backed up.

"Get out of our house! Get out now!" Marshall yelled at his father.

Brandon was not ready to give up and run. He reached for the box again.

"I need some money. I bought that stuff for your mother. It's mine and I plan on taking it when I leave. And I'm not leaving without it. Give it here," Brandon said.

"It's not yours. It's Mom's," Marshall said as he shoved the box in a dresser drawer.

Brandon was enraged by Marshall's defiance. He grabbed him and shoved him against the wall. Marshall grabbed his father's shirt and kicked him in the groin. Brandon doubled over in pain. Standing up again he punched Marshall in the face. Marshall staggered backward tripping over his mother's body and fell on the bed. As Brandon reached for him again, sirens could be heard coming down the road. As the sound of the sirens got closer Brandon backed up and ran out the bedroom door, passing Sean standing there with the phone pressed against his chest.

Marshall sat up and looked at Sean. His face was white and fear was in his eyes as he looked at his mother's form on the floor. Tears began to stream down his face. Marshall scrambled off the bed and knelt at his mother's side. He bent down to her face and was relieved to find slight breathing from her. He looked up at Sean just as he heard someone calling from the front door.

"Hello, Police. Everything okay here?"

Marshall ran to the door which was standing wide open.

"My dad was just here. He hit my mother. She's unconscious," Marshall told the officer.

The officer came in and looked over Amy. He made a call for an ambulance.

"Is there someone you can call. Your mother needs to go to the hospital. I think she'll be fine but we need for her to be checked out," the officer told Marshall.

"My grandparents live right down the road. I'll call them to come get my little brother. I'm going to the hospital with my mother," Marshall replied.

Before the call could be made however, Sarah and Loren arrived.

"I heard the siren and saw a police car pull in here. What's happened," Sarah asked.

She then saw Amy lying on the floor.

"Oh my God. What happened," she said kneeling over her daughter.

"Dad was here. He hit her and she fell and hit her head on the bed frame," Marshall explained.

Sarah pushed the hair from Amy's face. When she pulled her hand away there was blood on her hand. When Sean saw the blood on his grandmother's hand he began screaming and crying. Loren pulled him to his chest and began trying to soothe him.

"It'll be okay. Your mom will be just fine. It's just a cut from the bed," he said into Sean's hair.

"Why won't she wake up? Why is she just laying there? Make her wake up," Sean sobbed as he clung to his grandfather.

The ambulance arrived and the attendants were escorted into the room. They assured that Amy was breathing normally and her pulse was good. They loaded her on a gurney and into the ambulance. Marshall insisted that he was going with his mother. Sarah said she would lock up the house and they would follow the ambulance to the hospital.

As the ambulance pulled out on the road, Marshall took his mother's hand. He bent over her and began praying. The attendants did not try to push him away.

"God, please take care of my mother. Please make sure she is okay. Don't let anything be wrong with her. Sean and I still need her. She still has work to do for you. Please God, take care of my mother. Please, please don't let anything happen to her."

Marshall wept as he prayed. He wanted to hate his dad. He wanted his dad to know fear and hurt like they had to because of him. Marshall knew that those feeling were not what God would want but he had a hard time feeling otherwise. It was hard to feel forgiving toward the person who had hurt his mother.

"God, please don't let me hate my dad. Don't let me be unforgiving. Help me to be like Christ, to be like you want me to be. Please make my mother okay. Let her wake up and be okay," he sobbed.

As in an answer to prayer, Amy moaned. She began stirring and opened her eyes. She looked into Marshall's tear streaked face.

"Son, what's wrong," she asked.

Amy tried to sit up and as she did so the ambulance attendants pushed her back down gently.

"You need to lie down, ma'am," one of the attendants told her.

"What's going on? God, my head hurts. Why does my head hurt so bad?" she asked.

"Mom, don't you remember? Dad hit you and you fell and hit your head on the bed," Marshall said.

"What? I don't remember. Where are we? Where's Sean?"

Amy began to get upset when she realized that Sean was not there.

"Sean's fine. He's with Gram. They're coming to the hospital."

"The hospital? Why are they going to the hospital. What happened?"

"They're going to the hospital because that's where we're going. You're in an ambulance. You were unconscious, Mom. Your head is bleeding."

Amy looked a bit confused. Before she could ask any more questions the ambulance stopped and the doors opened. She was taken out and pushed into the hospital emergency room. She watched the lights overhead pass and tried to figure out what happened. She remembered Brandon coming in but didn't remember what had transpired. The ambulance attendants lifted her off the gurney and began speaking to someone she couldn't see.

A face appeared over hers. The doctor looked in her eyes with his little light.

"How are you feeling?" he asked.

"My head hurts something fierce. Other than that, I guess I'm okay."

"Do you know what happened?"

"Not really. My son said my ex-husband hit me and I fell and hit my head on the bed. But I don't remember it."

"Well, it looks like he did a good job. You're going to have a beautiful shiner come tomorrow. And you have a pretty good concussion by the looks of things. We need to run a few tests. I'm going to keep you here tonight and we'll see how things go tomorrow after the tests. I'm sure you'll be fine but you'll probably have that headache for a few days. Is this your son?" he asked, indicating Marshall.

"Yes, my oldest."

"Well, he'll probably have a matching shiner. Have you spoken with the police?"

Amy looked at Marshall in the light of the emergency room. Sure enough, his left eye was swelling and turning blue.

"Marshall, you didn't tell me he hit you. Are you okay?"

"I'm fine. I got home and found you and Dad fighting. I walked into the room just as he hit you. I got your jewelry box from him. He didn't get anything. He hit me but I kicked him first. Sean called 911 just like you taught him. I guess we all forgot about Sean. But he saved the day. Dad heard the sirens and ran off. I talked a little to the police but I'm sure they want to talk to you."

"I'm not concerned about the jewelry. I just want to make sure you and Sean are okay."

"We're fine. He can stay with Gram until you come home."

"Where are you going to stay?"

"I'm staying here with you."

"You've got school tomorrow. You need to be in school. I'll be fine. Go home with Gram. I'll most likely be released tomorrow and be home when you get out of school. I appreciate you taking care of me. We have the weekend to get over this."

"I'm not leaving, Mom. I don't have anything tomorrow that I can't make up."

Amy realized that he was adamant about staying and relented. She was put in a room and Sean came in with Sarah and Loren. Sean looked relieved to see her awake.

"Are you okay, Mom?" he asked.

"I'm fine. I have a really bad headache but I'm okay. I hear you are a hero."

"A hero? I'm not a hero. I was scared and I cried."

"Just because you were scared and cried doesn't mean you're not a hero. Marshall said you called 911. It could have been much worse if you hadn't been so smart. I'm glad I have such a smart and brave son. You saved me and Marshall. You're my hero."

Sean grinned. "I did just like you taught me. I dialed 911 and gave the lady my address and told her I needed the police to come to my house. I told her my dad was beating up my mom. She said they would be right there. She told me I was smart because I knew my address and I knew what to do."

"She's right. You did good. I'm glad that you're my brother," Marshall told Sean.

Amy didn't think there could be a prouder child than Sean right now. While the situation was okay for now, she wondered what they would be in for next. As the police officer came in her room she wasn't sure exactly what to tell them. She didn't know where Brandon was or what he involved in. And she remembered little of the fight. Unfortunately she would have to rely on Marshall to help to fill in the blanks. The fact that he had to speak to the police about his father's attack broke Amy's heart. No child should have to do that, she thought.

Chapter Sixteen

A my was released from the hospital the next day. She had called her boss to let him know what had happened. He was concerned about her staying in her house without some means of protection. She assured him that everything would be okay. She hoped that it would be but did not let on that she had a small measure of fear hidden away. The doctor had given her several prescriptions for her concussion. Marshall had taken them and gotten them filled. He had even paid for them himself. Amy felt that she was putting too much responsibility on him. She abhorred the fact that he had been forced to stand up to his father and been hit in the process. He on the other hand was glad he could do it.

She lay on her sofa that afternoon and pondered what the outcome of this latest battle would be and what would change in their lives. She had a long talk with Marshall earlier as they were on their way home from the hospital. He said he had prayed for forgiveness because he was so angry at his father he wanted to hurt him. He told her that he was trying to do what was right but it was really hard under the circumstances. Amy said she was sure God understood and for him to continue to pray about it. She told him she too had to pray about the same thing. Marshall seemed to appreciate the fact that she struggled with the same problem.

Later that afternoon after Marshall had gone to work and Sean was at his grandmother's house, Amy had finally given in and taken one of the pain pills prescribed by the doctor. She had tried to resist taking them because they made her sleepy. She found she was a little afraid to go to sleep. Fighting sleep, she was aroused by the ringing of the doorbell. Peering through the peep hole, she saw Dillon standing on her door step.

"Dillon, come in," she said, opening the door.

"Hey, nice shiner," he said, commenting on her black eye.

"Don't you like it? It's the new rage in body art," she said with a laugh.

"Alyssa told us what happened. The guy's a jerk for hitting a woman. More so his ex-wife and son. Are you okay?"

"I'm fine. It looks bad and I have an ugly headache but I'm really fine."

"Good. I'd hate to have to take him out. I was wondering if I could talk to you."

"Sure. What about?"

"Alyssa told me you were asking about my interest in Lacy. She didn't mean any disrespect to you by telling me. She said that others, including herself, was probably wondering the same thing. I think she's afraid I have an interest in a sixteen year old girl."

"So what is your interest in her? Not that it's really any of my business but I care about her."

"It's okay. My interest is not so much in the fact that she's a girl. I mean she's a pretty girl but she's young and still has a lot of growing up to do. The last thing she needs right now is some guy making a move on her. I know that. My interest, if that's what you want to call it, has more to do with the choice she's made. I know the guy that got her pregnant. I don't know him well, just casually. I saw them together and I asked him if she was old enough to be with him. He's over twenty-one and she didn't look more than seventeen at the most.

"He said she told him she was eighteen. I asked him if he believed it and he said it didn't matter how old she was if she was willing. I saw him later with another girl. I asked him where Lacy was and he said he'd gotten rid of her. She had told him she was pregnant and how old she really was. He said she was desperate and wanted him to marry her. He couldn't do that because he was already married for the same reason. He told her to get rid of it. He said he offered her money for an abortion and she turned it down. He told her either get rid of it or he'd get rid of her. She said she was keeping her baby. That was the last time they saw each other.

"I think at her age, like sixteen is so much younger than nineteen, the choice to keep her baby would be a difficult choice. She knows it will be hard and she's prepared to stand by her choice anyway. My parents don't know this but I got a girl pregnant nearly a year ago. The girl was a year older than me and she initiated our sexual relationship. I thought we were in love. I mean I really cared about her and thought she cared about me. She came to me one day and asked for some money. I asked her what she needed and she told me she was pregnant and wanted to get an abortion.

"I told her she didn't have to, that I would take care of her and the baby. She laughed and said she didn't want the baby. She'd only been having fun with me and she'd never wanted a permanent relationship with me. She wasn't into that and had already had two abortions. I didn't give her the money but I guess she got some from somewhere because she had the abortion. People see that tiny being as a thing and not a life. I remember when my mom was pregnant with Alyssa. I was pretty young and didn't understand much of what was going on but I remember her being sad about almost losing her baby.

"As Alyssa grew up, I loved her and loved having her around. I thought how sad life would have been to not have had her in my life. That's what I thought about when this girl told me she wanted to get rid of my baby. I had no way to stop her and I feel such grief when I think about the life that was destroyed by someone's selfishness. That child could have been such a joy to a loving parent. But he was never given a chance at life. That's why I care about Lacy. Because she chose to give life and not destroy it. I will support her in anyway I can. Does that make sense?"

Amy thought about what Dillon had told her. She realized he was simply celebrating with Lacy in the new life that would soon be born.

"It does. Thank you for telling me. I think in the long run she will be glad she made the choice she did. I lost a baby between Marshall and Sean. I think about that baby from time to time. I could not imagine purposely taking the life of an unborn child. Unfortunately, as you know, it happens all the time. My consolation is that my baby is with his Heavenly Father."

"Is that how you think of it? Does it make it easier? I hate to think my baby was just garbage somewhere."

"That's exactly how I think of it. It does make it easier. God knew each of us before we were born. If we, as sinful as we are, were meant to be with him in paradise why would he not take those innocent babies too?"

"So you think my baby is in heaven?"

"Absolutely. He's probably there playing with my baby."

Amy could see the tenderness in Dillon's eyes. "I like that idea. I had never thought of God as our Heavenly Father. He always seemed so abstract to me. It was hard to get a grasp on the idea of this spiritual being watching and judging us from above. I just didn't see how this 'God of love' could let us destroy ourselves, to let so much horror exist in this world he created. It just never made sense to me."

"God is a God of love. He has given us the choice to make something good in this world. Our choice though has often been to do something bad, to be destructive for selfish and self-centered reasons. It's like your friend. She had an opportunity to give life and chose instead selfishness that destroyed life. That's what we do as humans. The only way to overcome that humanness is to live a life in God. He gives us the strength to make the hard choices, to chose his life over our life. It's hard sometimes, a lot of times. But in the end we'll be richly rewarded.

"I was asked once if when I got to the end of life and found out that there was no God, after living like there was all my life, wouldn't I be disappointed. I would have missed out on so much because I lived this kind of life. I asked my friend what would I have missed? Did I miss being a drunk or drug abuser, a murderer, a sexual pervert? I don't see how I missed anything. And what did it hurt me to be kind and forgiving to people? Which kind of person would she rather have as a friend, a Christian who strives to be charitable, understanding, and loving or a drunken thief that can't be trusted? And what would happen if I lived my life like there was no God and found out at the end that there was? I'd rather live a godly life than an ungodly one than risk making the wrong choice and end up in hell."

"Yeah, that makes sense. But those of us that have messed up already don't have much choice. I wished I'd given it more thought when I was growing up. I was afraid I'd miss out on life if I lived for God. Alyssa has dedicated her whole life to Him. She'll make it to heaven for sure. I wish I had her dedication."

"Dillon, your life if not over. You have as much chance as she does. All you have to do is make a commitment to God. Ask him to forgive you of your sins and invite him into your heart. The only time it's too late is when your dead."

"But I've done so many bad things. I know you think I'm just nineteen and how much bad could I have done already. I told you about one mistake I made but there are plenty others."

"But none is unforgivable. Remember the thief that hung on the cross next to Jesus? He was hanging there dieing for his crimes. He acknowledged Jesus as the Son of God and asked that he remember him in heaven. Jesus told him he would be with him in heaven that day. He forgave him of his sins as he was about to die, even after living his entire life in sin. Right there on the cross. See, Dillon. You have an opportunity every day to live for God. He knows we will make mistakes in our lives but he is willing to forgive us if we ask him. Just as your earthly father does, just as you would have done for your own child. All you have to do is ask him. He loves you so much. Give him a chance to show you."

Dillon nodded his head. "I'll do that. Thanks. I've got to run. I'm glad I talked to you. I got some things for Lacy, for the baby. Can I give them to you to give to Lacy for me? I don't want anyone to misconstrue my intentions. I guess, if you can, explain why I'm not giving them to her in person. I'm sure she'll understand."

"I'll explain it to her. But if you want to give them to her in person, we're having a get together at my mother's in a couple of weeks. We have some things we want to give her besides what we have for the shower at church. Loren made her a beautiful cradle and Mom and I made some things to go in it. Since it will be ladies only at the church shower, we planned this so Loren and the boys could be there. Alyssa is coming so why don't you join her? I'm sure she'd appreciate your being there."

"Are you sure you don't mind? I hate to horn in on things. I want to be there when the baby is born but don't know how to handle that."

"Handling it will be easy. Just come with Alyssa. Or just come. You're her friend. I will expect to see you at our shower. Okay?"

"Okay. Thanks so much for understanding. And thanks for helping me understand about God. I guess I should talk to my parents. I avoided it in the past because I didn't want to buy into the religion thing just because that's what they were into. I wanted to make my own choice. At least that's what I told myself. I really wanted to indulge in life. And it wasn't much of a life. I messed up. But I know I can be forgiven and do better. I'll see you at church Sunday, if you come. I'm sure everyone will understand if you don't since you have that new body art."

Amy waved him out the door. She was glad he had come by. And she hadn't given any thought about church on Sunday. She and Marshall would both be sporting a black eye. She didn't know how many knew about the incident. Her pastor had called earlier to check on her so somehow the news had reached him. She kicked back on the sofa and thought she'd give in to sleep. At least her head had stopped hurting. She drifted off to sleep without much more thought.

She was awakened a short time later with the ringing of the phone. It took her a moment to realize what the noise was that had awaken her.

"Hello," she said, still a little groggy.

"Amy Alexander?" a woman's voice asked.

"Yes. Who is this?" she asked.

"Sylvia Porter," was the reply.

"Sylvia Porter? You called before. My mother said you'd called. Do I know you?"

"Not really. We've never met. I'm Brandon's mother."

Amy was fully awake now. "Brandon's mother? Brandon's not here. He and I divorced a while back."

"Yes, I know. He has stayed with me off and on since the divorce. But I haven't seen him for a couple of weeks."

"Oh. Well, what can I do for you?"

"I just wanted to talk to you. I wanted to find out what happened to him, how he got so far into drugs."

"That I can't answer. I really don't know. He told me it was to help him to concentrate at work or relax him because he was so stressed out. But I don't think that's the truth. He was running with some woman and she introduced him to it. I don't know much about it. It was usually during an apology after he beat me up that a few details come out. I quit caring why a long time ago."

"I understand. I didn't know he beat you up. He told me you had an affair and threw him out. He said that he lost his job after you threw him out and he stayed on the streets. He turned to drugs because he was so despondent about losing his family. I believed him, for a while. Then I found out he was stealing from me. I told him he would have to clean himself up and get off drugs or he would have to find some place else to stay. He flew into a rage and slapped me so hard it made my ears ring. He told me I was just like you, selfish and uncaring. I saw a different side of him and I was afraid so I made him leave. But I felt so bad, especially since I wasn't there for him like I should have been when he was growing up.

"I went to find him but didn't know where to look. That's when I first called your house. But I found him and that's why I'm calling you now. Apparently he attacked you yesterday and has been running from the police. He was sighted and was running from a couple of officers and ran in front of a car. He's hurt pretty bad and the doctors are having a hard time taking care of him because of the drugs in his system.

"He knows that his situation is grim and has been asking to see you and the boys. Could I beg of you to come to the hospital? Not necessarily the boys if you're not comfortable with it. Please, Amy?"

"What do you mean, his situation is grim? What is grim?"

"It means he may not pull through. He was hurt pretty badly."

"I'll come up there. I'm going to talk to Marshall at work and let him know. I don't think Sean will want to see his father. But I'll talk to him. Where do I need to go?"

"He's in ICU. I'll be here."

"Okay."

As Amy hung up the phone she wondered what Brandon wanted from her. She would like to refuse to see him but if he didn't make it she would be sorry later. She walked to her mother's house to help clear her head. How would she explain to Sean that his father wanted to see him after what had happened the day before? And what would Marshall's response be?

Chapter Seventeen

"No, I don't want to go," Sean yelled. "You can't go. Not after he hit you and made your head bleed. Please don't go, please."

Sean was very upset and Amy could not get him to understand that his father was no threat now.

"Sean, he can't hurt me now. Don't you understand, he's hurt real bad. The doctor said he may not live."

"I don't care. You can't go," he cried clinging to her.

"Son, I know you're afraid he'll hurt me again. But he can't. I have to go and see what he wants. I have to forgive him for what he has done. God wants me to do that, it's the right thing to do."

"I won't forgive him, I hate him. I won't forgive you if you go. I won't." Sean ran off and shut himself in the spare bedroom.

"Amy, you have to go. Sean will be okay. When you come back and he sees that you're okay, he'll come around. Go on and I'll talk to him," Sarah told her.

Reluctantly Amy left and went to the restaurant. She told Marshall what was going on. He told her he'd come to the hospital as soon as he got off from work. Amy headed to the hospital. She prayed that Brandon would be okay. As much hurt as he had dealt to her and her sons, she still wanted him to be okay. She parked and walked to the ICU. She saw a woman sitting in the ICU waiting room that could only be Brandon's mother, the resemblance was uncanny.

"Mrs. Porter?" she asked approaching the woman.

"Amy? It's good that you came. I guess the boys didn't want to come with you?" Sylvia Porter said, grasping her hand in greeting.

The two women sat down but Sylvia did not let go of Amy's hand.

"Sean was very upset. He refused. I don't know that I blame him with what he witnessed yesterday. Marshall is coming when he gets off from work. How is Brandon doing?"

"Not good. He comes in and out of consciousness. He has a lot of internal injuries. The doctors are having a hard time with his medication because of the drugs he already had in his system. They asked me what he was on but I have no idea. I don't know how he got into this situation. I mean the drugs, I don't know how he got involved with drugs. He called me out of the blue about a year ago and said he was having problems and needed to borrow some money. Said I owed it to him to help him get out of this fix. I didn't give him any, not after the last time."

"The last time? You've given him money before? He told me he had lost contact with you years ago."

"We've never lost contact. We didn't pursue any contact but we always knew where the other was. We've spoken over the years but it was always unpleasant. Brandon would call me up and ask if Harold was still making my life miserable. Harold didn't make my life miserable but he did make it difficult when it came to Brandon. But Brandon had no reason to complain, it was Harold's money that sent him to college."

"Brandon told me he went to college on student loans. For years he held out several hundred dollars a month from his paycheck that he said was to pay off his loans."

"Well, dear we were both snookered. Harold told me shortly after we were married that Brandon was stealing from me. We had a big row over it. I didn't believe Brandon would do such a thing. He had never given me much trouble, just the regular boy stuff. But Harold swore it was the truth. I asked Brandon about it and he was so angry. I had never seen such anger. The idea that I would even listen to Harold's accusation enraged him. The incident created a riff between us and we never got close again. If I asked him about anything, he flew into a rage. There were plenty of things that I began to notice come up missing, money out of my purse, jewelry, silver. He would throw things and break things, he even punched the walls.

"As he got older I grew to be afraid of him. Harold didn't like him in the house and was willing to pay for him to go to college just to get him out. It was peaceful once he was gone. But I felt guilty for the distance between us. I tried to make amends. Every time I spoke to him, he asked for money. So I saw him less and less. Before he graduated from college, he told me he was getting married and I was so happy for him. I wanted him to be happy. He asked if he could borrow the money for a honeymoon.

"I didn't want to ask Harold for the money, I never told him I gave Brandon money because it would have made him angry. So I took some out of my savings, an account Harold set up for me if I wanted to decorate the house or something, and gave it to Brandon. He said it wouldn't get him far and make him look like he couldn't afford to take care of his wife. I told him I was sorry but it was all I had. I asked about coming to the wedding but he said it was going to be a small private affair."

"Brandon and I didn't go on a honeymoon. He had just started a new job and couldn't take off. I mean we went to a motel for the weekend but it was nothing elaborate. But we had a nice church wedding."

"Yes, I know. I found out about it when the announcement came out in the paper. I began to suspect that the money was not being used for the things he had asked for it for. There were just too many things that didn't make sense. I finally stopped giving him any money. He was angry and stopped calling. I kept track of him though. I called him when Marshall was born and asked if I could come over and see the baby. He told me no, that you didn't want me to be part of the family since I had not been supportive. I was really hurt by that. I cried for days over that. Harold said he doubted you'd said that. I didn't know what to think."

"I would never had cut you off from your grandchildren."

"I know that now. I don't know what was going on in Brandon's head, what he needed the money for. He told me he was behind on his car payment, several times. He told me the boys were sick, you were sick, the house needed repairs. I just couldn't believe the things he told me but I worried that they were true. What if because I didn't give him some money, one of the boys were suffering or worse."

"I don't know why he asked for money. He made good money at work and I worked off and on as the boys came along and started school. We never needed for anything. If the car payment got behind, I never knew about it. That's not to say it didn't happen. By the time we got divorced I had to work full time just for us to make ends meet and Brandon was making really good money. I don't know how long he had been involved in drugs before I found out. And that was an accident.

"The boys and I had left to go to a birthday party for a friend of Sean's. After the party we were going to the mall for Christmas shopping. But Sean had had an accident and I had to go by the house to clean him up. We got home and I cleaned Sean up. I walked in the bedroom to let him know what was going on and found him with cocaine. He hadn't even realized we had come in. I didn't know what to do so I grabbed the boys and left. We stayed gone all day. That night when we got home I sent the boys straight to bed. He was waiting for me. He told me he was under a lot of stress and it helped him keep going.

"After that Brandon changed. He was angry all the time. The boys were afraid of him and would run to their rooms when he came home. Usually it was late so they would just go to bed. He would find a fault and berate me. After a while he started hitting me. I never knew what to expect. I asked him what was wrong and he would say it was me. I tried to stay out of the way and that made him angry. I tried to be attentive and that made him angry. I found out he was having an affair with a woman at his office. But I didn't care, I was relived because it meant he was home less. Finally he moved out and said he wanted a divorce. I was glad it was over.

"Then a couple of weeks ago he started calling and asking for money. He talked to Marshall on the phone first. We tried to keep Sean from inadvertently answering the phone but he did anyway. It scared Sean so bad. Brandon told him he should get rid of us because we were keeping him from having any money. I guess he was referring to the child support. Then his girlfriend took Sean from school trying to get me to give them money. I never expected him to show up at the house like he did. I guess he had finally gotten desperate. I know he was fired from his job at least six weeks ago. I don't know what all has gone on with him."

"I'm surprised you're here at all. I don't know if I would be if I were in your situation, not after all he did to you and your children."

"I loved Brandon. He is the father of my children. Somehow he lost control of his life. If he truly does not make it, if his condition is that bad, I don't want him to die without knowing forgiveness."

"Forgiveness? I'm not sure he deserves forgiveness."

"None of us deserve it. None of us are faultless. I've lived my life as a Christian and part of that life is to forgive those that trespass against us. If Jesus could forgive those who took his life, I can forgive one who made mine difficult. It's what I'm trying to teach my sons, especially Sean."

"That would be mighty difficult, to forgive someone that trespassed the way he did."

"God never told us it would be easy. He just said do it."

Deep in thought, silence stretched between them as they thought about the conversation. A nurse appeared reminding them of where they were.

"You can go in now," she said.

Amy took Sylvia's hand and together they went into the unit to see Brandon. Amy was not sure what to expect. As she entered the small cubicle, the flashing lights and beeping machines caught her eye. Brandon was hooked up to several pieces of equipment and had tubes sticking out of him in several places. His head was bandaged but what she could see was discolored, much worse than hers. She thought he was sleeping and was unaware of their presence. A moan told her otherwise. She leaned over his face and saw one eye slightly open. The other was swelled shut.

"Brandon? Can you hear me," she said quietly.

Another moan was her answer. She thought it sounded like a yes. She leaned a little closer.

"His jaw is broken," Sylvia said.

"Oh," Amy replied to her.

She began to straighten up and Brandon moaned again. She leaned back down. He seemed to look at her swollen face and the deep purple bruise around her eye. Brandon moaned again but it sounded as if he was trying to talk to her.

"What is it," she asked. She had a hard time understanding what he wanted. After a few moments she realized he was asking about Marshall and Sean.

"Marshal will be here later, after he gets off from work. Sean wouldn't come," she told him.

He closed his eye for a moment. A tear slid down his cheek. A few more moans and grunts from Brandon Amy took as an apology.

"It's okay. I forgive you," she said.

Never had she wanted to see him in such a condition. Even though her face hurt from his punch the evening before, she did not want to see him suffering in such a way. She knew that most people wouldn't understand what she felt. But she knew that he wasn't an evil person, he was simply lost and afraid. Amy stroked his cheek, wiping the wet streak away. Another followed as Brandon received her forgiveness. The compassion Amy felt had nothing to do with the love she had felt for him as her husband. It was what someone would feel looking at a wounded child. His body may never heal but Amy wanted him to feel comfort should this be the last contact he would have on earth.

"Brandon, remember when we talked about God years ago? You wanted to know if he was real or just a fairy tale? He is real and he wants you to know he loves you. You're his child and he loves you very much. I know you never meant to hurt me or the boys. I know you were hurting inside. And God knows. He is willing to forgive you if you just ask him. Won't you do that? Ask him, Brandon. Let his love fill you with peace."

Amy watched as his face sought the truth in her eyes. He closed his eye and his lips moved silently in prayer. He looked at her again and smiled. Amy was glad that she'd had the opportunity to lead him to the Lord, even though it may be at the end of his life. He closed his eye and appeared to settle into sleep. The nurse came in and told them their time was up. Amy and Sylvia went back to the waiting room to wait for the next visitation hour.

"Amy, do you really believe all that? I've heard that before but it just doesn't make sense. If God loved Brandon why is he laying in that bed?" Sylvia asked.

"I believe it. What's more important is that right now Brandon believes it. He never didn't believe it, he just didn't want to bend to God's will. That's why he's in that bed. He wanted all the pleasures that come in this world without any responsibility for his actions. We all have to pay the price for sinful indulgence."

"So you believe that all we have to do is say I'm sorry to God and everything is okay?"

"No, it's not really that simple. We have to confess that Jesus is the son of God and that he died for our sins. I'm sure you've heard all that. We have to realize that we live in sin and that sin separates us from God. We have to ask for forgiveness for those sins. We may not think we live in sin. We may give to charity and feed the poor. We may not curse or drink or commit murder or any of those things we naturally think of when we think of sin. But if we are not living for God, we are living for ourselves. We have put ourselves before God, make an idol of ourselves, and that is a sin. We have to be forgiven and put him back in control. That is actually the easy part. If we are sincere, we have to continue to walk in Him, allow him to have control over our hearts, minds and body. That's where so many lose it, they don't let him keep control because they think they are missing something. And they end up doing just that. They miss God's gifts to us and the opportunity to live with him at the end of this life."

Amy and Sylvia sat quietly, pondering those words in their own way. Both jumped when the doctor entered the room.

"Mrs. Porter? I've checked on your son. He's slipped into a coma. His systems are beginning to shut down. I need you to make a difficult decision. He may not hang on too much longer. Will you want us to resuscitate him if he quits breathing?" he asked kneeling before her.

"What would happen if you did?" Sylvia asked.

"He'd have to be put on life support. His heart is damaged from the accident. He has a ruptured lung, a broken back and other internal organ damage from the drugs. The decision is yours. I'll let you think about it but don't think to long."

The doctor left the room and Sylvia turned to Amy.

"What do you think? I mean, I know he's hurt bad, that his life will never be the same. But life support. That means he won't really be living, right?"

"Pretty much. It's not what Brandon would want," Amy replied.

Even though he was no longer her husband and the choice was not hers to make, it was hard to choose between the options. Sylvia got up and walked out of the room. She was gone about ten minutes and came in and sat down. She looked like she was in shock.

"I talked to the doctor. He said it was the right choice, to not resuscitate him if he quit breathing. While we were standing at Brandon's door….." Sylvia began to sob. "While we were standing right there…he's gone. He just stopped breathing."

Sylvia's grief was unabashed. Amy, crying herself, pulled Sylvia into her arms. After a few moments Sylvia pushed away and looked at Amy.

"Can we go to the chapel and pray? Show me how to talk to God. Help me like you helped Brandon," Sylvia said.

Amy helped her to her feet and they walked to the chapel together.

Chapter Eighteen

A my didn't have the opportunity to deal with her feelings concerning Brandon's passing for several days. She wasn't even sure what she should be feeling. She had sat with Sylvia for several hours at the hospital as she tried to get a grip on her feelings. Sylvia told her she had recently put her husband in a home because she could no longer care for him. He had been diagnosed with Alzheimer's disease and she had kept him at home as long as she could. He had wandered off several times and gotten lost, had turned the burners on the stove on and caught things on fire, and nearly overdosed on his medication when he had taken it thinking he hadn't yet.

As much as she had hated it, she had to put him in a home for his own sake. Now on the heels of that she had to deal with the loss of her son. As Amy had listened to Sylvia pour her heart out, she felt sorrow for Sylvia's double loss though not giving her personal feelings any thought. The next day was consumed with helping Sylvia make funeral arrangements, again putting off her dealing with the issue personally.

She talked to the boys about Brandon passing away. Sean was confused about what he was supposed to feel. He was sad that his father had died but he was relieved that he wouldn't have to be afraid anymore. Then he felt guilty for being relieved. Marshall was quiet on the matter. He just nodded his head but said nothing. Amy wasn't sure what was going on in his head. She was concerned that he was feeling guilt of his own for not seeing his father before he passed away. It was not until she walked into the room at the funeral home for visitation that she began to sift through her emotions.

Looking at him lying in his casket, she was saddened that his life choices took him from his family, saddened that whatever it was he had been looking for he did not find. He lived an unhappy life, searching for a magic potion that would bring him the joy and pleasure he thought life should have. All the while it was closer than he had ever imagined, found in the last moments of his life. She didn't feel though that she had lost her spouse. That feeling she had already passed through in the months preceding the divorce. She grieved that he would never see his sons grow up and become men and they in turn would not know a father's love and support.

As she stood there reflecting on Brandon's life, she felt a presence behind her. Turning she saw that Brandon's boss, Trevor Whitlow, had joined her beside the casket. Amy had met him several times in the past during office parties. She was surprised to see him at the visitation, especially since Brandon had been fired weeks before his accident.

"I'm sorry for your loss, Mrs. Alexander," he said.

"Thank you," she replied. "I was just thinking about his life trying, I guess, to figure out just what my loss was."

"What do you mean?"

"Well, you know Brandon and I were divorced?"

"Yes, I knew that. But from the look on your face, I believe you still cared for him. That if things could have worked out you would have stayed with him."

"I did care for him. I would much rather have been able to work things out, especially for the boys' sake. There would have been a lot we'd have to work out though. He had some issues that I didn't even know about. But it's hard to forget the years we had together, to think that now they don't matter. "

"They matter. They'll always matter. They were a part of your life. And your children's lives."

Amy smiled and looked at Mr. Whitlow's face. It was a gentle but sad face. He had always seemed kind to her though Brandon often put him down. He moved away when Sarah came to stand by her daughter.

"Who is that? I don't recognize him."

"Trevor Whitlow, Brandon's boss."

"Oh. It's nice that he came. I've been taking to Sylvia. She really needs a friend. She's been so consumed in taking care of husband, she has cut herself off from friends and family. I've convinced her to join my garden club. She'll be a nice addition. You know she studied horticulture? I also invited her to come to church and she said she would try. I hope she does, she seems so lost."

"I know. Her husband is in a home and her only child is gone. I think it's great that you've befriended her. Brandon always spoke badly of her but I think she's a good person. I wished I had met her long before now. Brandon wouldn't let me contact her, said she didn't approve of me though he never gave me a reason why. I asked him if she would want to get to know her grandchildren and he said she didn't want any part of them because of me. I think it was because he didn't want us to compare notes. They have missed a lot of years, Sylvia and the boys."

"Well, she has taken to Sean. She tried to talk to Marshall but he just sat there like a bump on a log. What's wrong with him anyway?"

"I don't know. He's been like that since I came home from the hospital. He never showed up there like he said he would. Maybe he feels guilty."

"I hope he gets over it. I don't like seeing him this way," Sarah said as she walked away.

Amy walked around and spoke to several people. She saw some she didn't know and wondered who they were. She thought they must have been coworkers though she didn't recognize any of them. A particular woman suddenly caught her eye. It was Brandon's girlfriend. Amy couldn't believe she was there. Lydia saw the direction of her look and sidled up to Amy.

"I'm sure she's disappointed," Lydia whispered.

"Why?" Amy asked.

"She was hoping to be the next Mrs. Alexander."

"What do you mean, hoping to be the next Mrs. Alexander? Was Brandon going to ask her to marry him, or had he already?"

"I don't know if he did but if he didn't she thought he would. She had written all over a napkin, a cloth napkin none the less, 'Mrs. Colette Alexander' several times. I had to throw the napkin away. I've seen her around, she always goes for the money."

"Brandon didn't really have any money. I mean we had a nice home and lived comfortably but he didn't have any excess."

"I doubt she knew that. Look, I've got to go but if you need anything just call me," Lydia said, giving her a hug.

After a while everyone had drifted out and Amy and Sylvia found that they were the only two in the room.

"I don't know if I can handle tomorrow," Sylvia said.

"I know, it'll be difficult. My father passed away right after Brandon and I were married. We had never been close but it still felt like a loss. Other than a school friend passing away in high school, that was the only time I had someone die that was close to me."

"It just seems like I'm losing my family. I have a sister but when Harold and I got married, we drifted apart. I haven't spoken to her in years. She's the only family I have left except Harold and he doesn't even know who I am anymore."

"You should call her and get reconnected. I'm sure she would love to hear from you. And you have me and the boys. We're your family aren't we?"

"You and the boys? Amy, you and Brandon were divorced. Why would you consider me family after all he did to you?"

"He may have been difficult to live with sometimes but there were also some good times. And I have the boys because of him and I wouldn't trade them for anything. I don't hold a grudge against him. If you don't mind, I would like to consider you family."

"I would like that very much. I just adore Sean. He is such a doll. He reminds me of Brandon when he was his age. I mean in his looks. Brandon was a very solemn child, but Sean is silly. He likes to laugh and that's good for a child. Marshall is more solemn like Brandon was."

"Marshall is not like that really. He has something on his mind or he would be more outgoing and warm. Teenage boys are a complete mystery to me. If you need me to come get you tomorrow let me know," Amy said as she and Sylvia walked out.

"Thank you. You are so dear to me. I'll see you tomorrow," Sylvia said, getting into her car.

Amy waved to her and walked to her car where Marshall and Sean were waiting. When she unlocked the doors, Sean crawled into the front seat and Marshall took the rear. That was very unusual, Any thought.

"I like Sylvia," Sean said. "She's nice. She said I could come and visit her whenever I liked. She has a dog named Maggie. I've always wanted a dog."

"Sean, she's your grandmother just like Gram is. Why are you calling her by her name?" Amy asked.

"She said I could. I don't know her like Gram, she said so. So she said I could call her Sylvia if I liked."

"I think that's rude. It's not her fault that you don't know her like Gram."

"No, it Dad's fault, just like everything else," Marshall said from the backseat.

"What do you mean, just like everything else? What else are you blaming on him?" Amy asked, somewhat indignant.

"Don't defend him. He's the one that messed everything up. He hit you for no reason and yelled at Sean and me for no reason. He moved out to be with that woman, the one that came to the funeral home tonight. I heard her telling everyone that would listen that she and Dad were supposed to get married, that she should have been the grieving widow, not you. Which was a stupid thing to say because you're not his widow, you weren't married any more. If he hadn't messed up his life, there would have been no grieving widow or ex-wife or even a funeral. You talk about us doing the right thing when a grown man can't even do the right thing," Marshall answered with anger rising in his voice.

"I had no idea you were so angry with your father. I'm sorry you've had to deal with all this but I hope you don't let it poison your life. You can see first hand what type of problems occur when you go down the wrong paths."

"Yeah, I can see," he mumbled.

When they arrived at the house Marshall went to his room and shut the door. Amy went to her room and kicked off her shoes.

"He's not acting much like a Christian, is he?" Sean asked her, startling her. She did not realize he had followed her into the room.

"No, he isn't. I'm glad you realize that. But you've been great. I know this is hard. A lot has happened this year hasn't it?"

"Yeah, and I hope it gets better. Stevie called this morning and asked if I could spend the night at his house. I told him I had to go to the funeral tomorrow so probably not. He asked if I could come over tomorrow. Can I?"

"I don't see why not. After the funeral you can go over there. But I don't know if I can take you. Do you think his dad can pick you up? And will you come back home tomorrow night? You've got to go to School on Friday."

"Mom, Friday there's no school. It's a teacher work day, remember? I'll call Stevie to see if his dad can pick me up."

Sean left the room to make his call. She was surprised to see how much maturity had taken place in him the last few months. Or was it the last few weeks? It seemed as if he and Marshall had changed places suddenly. A few minutes he was back with the phone.

"It's Stevie's dad. He wants to talk to you," Sean said handing her the phone.

"Hello," she said.

"Mrs. Alexander. I don't mind picking Sean up after I get off from work, if that works for you. And Stevie wants him to stay the night. He has a new race track he wants to show off. He can stay the weekend and come to church with Lacy and Stevie on Sunday, if that's alright."

"I forgotten tomorrow was a work day for everybody. I can bring him over later in the day. I was thinking about going to Brandon's mother's after the funeral. Our church has gotten together and is bringing food over there for her. It would be nice to think about more than just these circumstances for a change. And I'd like to see Lacy. How's she doing?"

"She's doing really well. I have to admit that I'm surprised. I expected her to be the same petulant child I saw the last time she was here. But she's happy and making plans for her baby. She's helpful around the house and continuing her studies. She's making really good grades. I guess I expected her to be a poor student for some reason. I suppose that's the idea we have about kids that get in trouble, that their not very bright."

"Yeah, you're right. We do seem to lump all kids into that category based on the actions they take. That's a lesson to us. Some are really bright kids that just missed a connection with someone."

"I still don't understand why she felt that I didn't care for her. I tried to stay close but she wouldn't have any part of me."

"You know that little girls identify with their fathers. A lot say they are going to grow up and marry their daddies. Even though they grow up and develop other relationships, they still think of themselves as daddy's only love. She felt that you had stopped loving her and was loving someone else, as if you could only love one person at a time."

"I guess. I'm sorry it took her present situation to help her find her way back to me. Not that I won't love her baby or think ill of her, but I fear it'll be more than she is prepared for."

"I think you're right but she'll manage and probably surprise you at how well she ends up doing. How are things with her and your wife?"

"Actually they're pretty good. Sometimes they act like teenagers together. Kim sits down with her and they talk and laugh. Lacy helps with Matthew, changing his diapers, feeding him and chasing after him. She has a hard time picking him up, he's a chunk and she's getting so big. But she says she wants to learn what to do." He began laughing. "The first time she changed a dirty diaper, she almost gagged. Especially when he stuck his hand in it. And then he peed all over her once. He flips over and runs away naked and she has to run him down. He ran off once and she caught him at the door just as Kim was paying the pizza delivery man. Lacy was so embarrassed. She's learning alright."

Amy chuckled at the baby's antics, remembering her own learning experiences. "Well, at least she won't be totally unprepared. You don't think that'll be too many kids for you and your wife with Sean there for the weekend?"

"No. It'll be okay. The boys will probably stay in Stevie's room all weekend playing. Though we might just throw Matthew in there with them. Stevie likes to play with his baby brother. He's kind of like a toy to Stevie."

"Okay then. I'll send plenty of clothes for him. But please call me if it gets to be too much trouble. I'll see you tomorrow."

Amy hung up the phone relieved that it was not her having to deal with a toddler and two step kids as well as a friend of one of them. She felt for poor Kim and hoped that her husband was not putting more on her than she could handle. She thought that would be another reason she'd not be walking down the isle again. At her age any man she met would most likely have children of his own. That was one prospect that scared her a lot.

Chapter Nineteen

As Amy listened to her pastor speak of the passing of life and the importance of knowing where one would spend eternity, she was grateful that she had an opportunity to lead Brandon to the Lord. She could not imagine coming to the end of life and facing death with fear and uncertainty. She could not imagine going through life with fear and uncertainty. Her mind turned to those that had never had the opportunity to hear about the love of God and his plan for salvation. She remembered thinking as a child about going to far away lands to bring the gospel to the lost, helping to meet their basic physical needs while bringing them hope of an eternity that would be without pain, hunger, sickness or grief.

As she got older the idea of going where there was no restrooms, running water and air conditioning caused her to reconsider those far off places. She thought about those a little closer to home that needed to know the love of Christ, the children in slums or the American Indian people. It better suited her to minister to them where the amenities were available. By the time she was in high school, she had forgotten about her desire to minister to the lost. She remembered it again when her marriage began to get rocky and felt like it was too late. Little did she realize that there were so many so close to her own doorstep that needed to be given the gospel.

At the close of the service, Amy gathered her sons and headed for the door. She was followed by her mother and step-father as well as Sylvia. As they waited for the casket to be loaded Amy saw Colette. She was weeping loudly and carrying on wildly. She was the epitome of the grieving widow, except she had not lost a husband. Amy noted that most of the small crowd was not buying her act. Finally the hearse was ready and the parade to the cemetery began. The crowd gathered around the burial site and once again the pastor spoke of this life and the one beyond this one.

"Romans six four through eight tells us, 'We were therefore buried with him unto his death in order that, just as Christ was raised from the dead through the glory of the Father, we too may live a new life. If we have been united with him like this in his death we will certainly also be united with him in his resurrection. For we know that our old self was crucified with him so that the body of sin might be done away with, that we should no longer be slaves to sin. Now if we died with Christ, we believe that we will also live with him," the pastor read from the Bible.

As he finished the service, the group passed Amy and her sons as well as Sylvia to express their condolences. Sylvia was grieving deeply, leaning on Marshall for support.

Colette stood off to the side and waited for everyone to leave. As the last person walked away, she marched up to Amy with an angry countenance.

"You are not his widow!" she all but screamed. "You are a pretender, you should not even be here."

"I'm a pretender?" Amy asked. She tried not to over respond and keep her words gentle. She found it was difficult. "I'm not pretending to be his widow. But I was his wife not long ago and he is the father of my children."

"I would have been his wife if it had not been for you. But you just wouldn't leave him alone. You kept pestering him to come back. You just wanted his money. I loved him!"

Amy thought the whole thing was ridiculous.

"I did not try to get him to come back. I had tired of getting hit by him and being yelled at by him. And he didn't have any money. I don't know what he told you but whatever it was apparently was far from the truth. I'm sorry he deceived you but you're not the only one he deceived."

Colette gave her an angry glare and walked away. Amy was sad that Sylvia had to witness the exchange. She turned to look at Sylvia and realized she too was sorry that it had taken place.

"I'm sorry my son was not more respectable," Sylvia said sadly.

She turned to walk to the car. Marshall and Sean waited to walk with her. She paused and turned back to Amy.

"Sarah has invited me to go to her house this afternoon. She said she arranged with the church to bring the food there. That way the rest of the family could enjoy it as well. Marshall has been kind and consented to drive me there. I hope you don't mind. I don't think I can go home and just sit there alone."

"No, that's fine. Probably a better idea anyway. I'll see you there."

Amy watched as Marshall assisted his grandmother in the car and Sean scrambled in with them. She was left standing there alone. She thought that was just as well. It gave her a few moments alone with her thoughts. As she walked to her car, she noticed Trevor Whitlow standing near.

"Mr. Whitlow. It was nice of you to come to the service," she said.

"Thank you. Please, call me Trevor," as he walked over and shook her hand. "I watched that scene with Colette. I don't know why she did that," he said.

"Do you know her?"

"Unfortunately, yes. She was a temporary at the office some time back. One of our secretaries was out for maternity leave and she filled in for her. We have a contract with one of the temporary agencies and they sent Colette. I never had a problem with anyone they'd sent in the past but Colette was a major problem. She could type and file and answer the phone but she didn't stay as busy as she needed to. She locked onto Brandon right away. She began spending more time in his office than necessary and I finally saw them together. I warned Brandon to stay away from her but he said his private life was his own. I reminded him that his actions in the office was not part of his private life and it was getting in the way of business.

"They cooled it after that but it didn't stop after hours. My secretary came back to work after six weeks and by that time Colette and Brandon were a hot item. He came in shortly after that and asked for a raise. He told me he needed it because his son was nearly at a driving age and the insurance would be higher for the cars and it would also allow for the boys to have more extra curricular activities at school. I suspected he needed it more for Colette than for his family so I denied him the raise. I didn't believe him because he had never seemed to care about their activities in the past."

"He didn't even know what activities they were involved in. We never discussed it and he never asked," Amy said.

"I'm sorry, Mrs. Alexander, about what he put you through. I never understood why men who had loving wives and families threw it all away. He never spoke bad about you in the office but he didn't hide his affair. He did seem unconcerned about his kids though. That was sad to me.

When I was younger, I was in a relationship with a lovely woman. We pretty much lived together but I didn't devote much time to her. I was so determined to get all the education I needed for the business world. Once I got it, I set out to be successful. My parents struggled for so much when I was growing up I was determined I wouldn't have to struggle for anything and neither would my family.

"I was so singled minded that I never noticed I was losing everything that really mattered. My girlfriend finally had enough of my distractions and left me. I thought she didn't understand what I was trying to do and just plunged ahead. Now here I am, as successful as I desired to be and no one to share it with. You can go home to your children and enjoy all the blessings they bring with their life. Even though you may struggle from time to time, you have a house full of love. I envy that. Brandon didn't know what he had."

Amy smiled. "Thank you. And you can call me Amy. It's nice to hear something positive about my disastrous marriage."

"Disastrous marriage or not, you have two fine sons. That's something to be grateful for."

"Yes it is. Would you like to join us at my mother's? Or do you have to get back to the office?"

"That would be intruding."

"No it wouldn't. You were acquainted with Brandon. Come meet his family."

"Are you sure? This is a pretty sad time. I saw the other woman, I'm not sure who she was, but she was grieving quite a bit."

"That was Brandon's mother. She missed a lot of years with her son, and unfortunately with her grandsons. Brandon and his mother had a falling out of sorts when he was young and he cut her out of his life, except to ask for money from time to time."

"He told me both his parents were deceased. I don't understand people that would say their parents were dead when they aren't. Why would they want to push their family out of their lives? I guess she has a lot to grieve for. I feel for her. I'll follow you to the house."

Amy led the way to Sarah's house. When she got there, she was surprised at the gathering. The few people at the funeral had apparently decided not to join them but there was a large crowd there none the less. The ones at the house were friends from her church and a few of her neighbors. Amy found Sylvia sitting with another woman she had not seen before. They appeared to be very close. Amy introduced Trevor to her parents and her sons. As Loren talked to Trevor Amy asked Sarah who Sylvia was talking to.

"That's her sister, Stella Runnels. She flew in this afternoon. She called the church to find out where Sylvia lived. The pastor didn't know but he told her we would be gathering here after the funeral. She came straight here from the airport. Did Sylvia tell you she and her sister were twins?" Sarah asked.

"Twins? I had no idea. And she's been cut off from her sister since she married Harold. What a shame."

"Stella scolded her for not staying in touch. They've been sitting together catching up on each other's lives. Imagine, with twins running in the family, you could have had twins yourself."

Amy looked at her mother. "You know when I was pregnant with the Marshall the doctor had thought at one time I was carrying twins. Brandon didn't react when I told him it may be twins. I was scared to death. Now I know why, he knew twins ran in the family. You know once the boys start having children, they could produce twins as well."

Marshall and Sean looked shocked at their mother's statement.

"I'm not having twins," Sean said, shaking his head.

"I don't think the choice is yours," Trevor said with a laugh.

"Who's is it?" Sean asked.

"God's. You take what he gives you," Trevor answered.

Sean shook his head again and walked away. Amy tasted a few of the things that had been brought over. Sean began to get antsy and she knew he was ready to head over to Stevie's. She told her mother she was going to head out and would see her later. Trevor caught her at the door and told her he had some things at the office that belonged to Brandon. He asked if he could bring them by later. She told him that would be fine and pointed out her house. Sean was waiting for her in the car.

"Marshall left and went to Alyssa's," Sean informed her.

"I know. He's helping her get some stuff together for Lacy's baby shower at the church."

"I thought we was having one at Gram's."

"We are. It's going to be next Friday night and then we're having one at the church for just the ladies the next day."

"Can Stevie come to the party at Gram's house?"

"Sure. It's a party for his sister. I'm sure Stevie's dad and step-mom will come so I would expect Stevie to be there. Listen, while your at Stevie's house this weekend, you need to remember that you're a guest and behave your self. Don't make any messes and don't be too loud. Remember there's a baby in the house."

"I know. I know," he said as they pulled into the driveway. "I will be good, I promise. Can I call you while I'm at Stevie's, just to make sure you're okay?"

"Sure you can. Just ask to use the phone. I love you." she said giving him a hug.

"I love you too. Bye."

157

She watched her son run across the yard and wait at the door. Stevie opened the door and the two boys waived her off. They disappeared inside the house. Amy backed out and headed for her home. When she arrived, she thought it was very quiet without any of the kids around. She suspected that she should get used to it since the boys were growing up and developing interests elsewhere. She changed clothes and straightened up the house a little. She thought about Sylvia and the years she had lost with those she loved, her twin sister, her son and her grandsons. She felt sorry for her and hoped somehow those years could be made up for. The boys had taken to her and it appeared she and her sister were well on the way of getting caught up.

The door bell rang and when she opened the door, Trevor was standing on her step with a box in his arms.

"Come in. I didn't expect you to bring his things today," she said.

"We've hired someone to replace Brandon so we had to clean his office out. I thought he would come back and get his things but he didn't."

"I can't imagine what he had there," she said as she began to look through the box.

There were pictures of the boys when they were still pretty young. She was surprised to see the pictures but not that they weren't recent photos. Most of the items were basic office type items but she had never seen them before. There were several plaques Brandon had received for a good job performance and a bowling trophy. She didn't know he bowled. At the bottom of the box was a laptop computer. She didn't know Brandon had owned one.

"Is this computer Brandon's?"

"I guess so. It doesn't belong to the office. It's a good laptop. I saw him use it a few times. He hadn't had it very long, I don't think. You might want to look through the files. I'm afraid he might have some information on it that might not be good for the boys to see. I came in his office one day and he had some pretty explicit pictures he had taken off the internet on it."

"Yeah, I might better do that. If it's a good computer, Marshall may want to have it. He has a desktop computer but it's old. I got it at a garage sale several years ago. I need to get him some better computer equipment before he heads off to college. I really appreciate you bringing this stuff to me. I could have come to the office and picked it up."

"I didn't mind. It gives me an opportunity to talk to you. You know, I had an older brother that went down the same path as Brandon. He hated the way we had to live when we were growing up. He got involved in drugs because of the money. When he came home for holidays, he always argued with our parents over his lifestyle choice. My parents were ashamed of what he did. He had no remorse about selling drugs to kids even if it killed them. His bottom line was money. It's all he cared about. He got killed when a buy went bad. I guess we make poor choices when we don't think about what we're doing and how it will effect our lives down the road."

"I'm trying to get the boys to understand that. Even what may seem like a small decision could have major effects on our lives as we get older. There is a cause and effect for everything we do. And I try to get them to understand that many of those choices will also effect other people in our lives. I think Marshall is beginning to understand. Sean is still young but I'll keep trying to pound it in his head."

"I'm sure he'll come around. You've got some smart kids. I talked to Marshall a little at your mother's. He's angry and I think that's understandable after all that's happened recently."

"Angry? Why would he have a reason to be angry?"

"I think part of it is that he's humiliated by his father's actions. And maybe he's afraid that he is more like his father than he would like to be. Brandon was a pretty smart guy despite where he ended up. He had great potential. Marshall said that if his dad had been a nicer person he'd like to have spent time with him. He said they had a few talks and were a lot alike in the way they saw things and felt about things. So he may be afraid that he'll be more like in dad in the bad ways too. And I know he's pretty mad about the way his dad treated you and Sean."

"I never knew Brandon and Marshall talked though I don't know why. I guess from time to time Brandon would go to the store or something and would take Marshall with him. I mean I remember it happening but I guess I never thought about them talking. I didn't have any kind of relationship with my dad growing up so I don't really know what I may have missed or what my kids have missed. I never thought that they wanted to have a relationship with their dad. He was always so angry we really just steered clear of him. I guess Marshall wanted it more than I thought. I'm glad you pointed it out to me."

"A man needs a man to talk to sometimes just like a woman needs another woman. I know Marshall was young but he still needed a man. It's a shame Brandon wasn't there for him more."

As they were talking Marshall came in.

"Mom? Oh, hi Mr. Whitlow," Marshall said, shaking Trevor's hand.

"Hello, Marshall. I brought your dad's things from the office. He never came to pick them up after he was fired."

"That's nice of you. What did he have?"

"Look at this computer. It looks pretty new. I thought you could use it. What do you think?" Amy said handing the laptop to her son.

"What do I think? I think it's pretty nice. I could put that computer program on it that I got for my birthday. It won't go on that old computer. Can I really have it? It's probably expensive. Don't you want to keep it, Mom?"

"I don't need it. I can use the old computer. You'll need it, especially when you go to college."

"We'll have to get a new printer. The old one won't hook up to this."

"I may be able to help you there. I have one at home that I don't use. I got a new computer and upgraded my printer. How about I work a deal?" Trevor asked.

"What kind of deal?" Marshall asked.

"I'm not sure yet. I'll have to get back to you on that. Why don't you come by my house one day and we'll look at some of the other computer equipment and see what else I can get rid of. I thought about giving some of it to my employees but I don't have a lot and if I give to some of them the others will be offended. I'd rather give it to someone who could really use it."

"I don't know. We're not beggars," Marshall said, somewhat angry.

"No, you're not. And I'm not planning to just give it to you. I was thinking about having you work it off," Trevor responded.

"I have a job," Marshall replied.

"I'm aware of that. I've been to the restaurant and seen you working. I was thinking about having you help me teach other youngsters how to use computers. I work with an after school youth program. Many of these kids come from pretty poor homes and are behind in their school work. They don't have computers in their homes and we help them do their homework, things they can't do at home without a computer. But we have to teach them how to use the computers first. We only meet with them two days a week. The rest of the time they have other instructors working with them with their math and reading. What do you think?"

"Sounds okay. I'll have to work it around my work schedule though."

"That's fine. So we have a deal?"

"Sure. When do you want me to come by your house?"

"That's up to you. When do you want to look at the rest of the stuff?"

Marshall grinned. "Soon."

"Anytime then. I'll see you later," Trevor said, shaking Marshall's hand and nodding to Amy.

Marshall looked like he had just won the lottery as he stroked his new computer.

Chapter Twenty

Marshall headed over to Trevor's house the following Friday afternoon. Lydia had given him the evening off to give another waiter an opportunity for Friday night tips. Business was picking up with the new entertainment and some of the employees wanted to reap the benefits. Marshall said he'd be back by dinner time as he was heading out the door so he could join her at Lacy's shower that evening. Amy headed to her mother's to get ready for the shower.

Amy and Sarah worked to make things perfect for the soon-to-be new mother. Lacy and her family arrived on time with Sean in tow. He was spending a lot of time at Stevie's house but James said it helped Stevie to feel more at home there. Sean wanted to show Stevie the baby cradle but Amy reminded him that it was a surprise for Lacy and had to be kept covered. The boys settled on trying to get in everyone's way. Alyssa and Dillon showed up burdened with gifts Dillon had gotten for the baby. As the shower got underway, both Alyssa and Amy kept watching the door for Marshall.

Lacy was thrilled with the cradle.

"I can't believe you made this for me. It's so beautiful," she said, as tears flooded her eyes.

As she sat opening her gifts, the baby began kicking. Stevie wanted Sean to feel the baby move. They would squeal with laughter at each kick. Lacy, on the other hand, looked pained. She had gotten so big Amy didn't think there was any more room for the baby to grow. And she still had nearly a month to go. As the shower ended, James loaded up his daughter's gifts as she hugged everyone and thanked them repeatedly. James assured Amy that Sean was just fine for the weekend and the guys were planning a trip to the arcade the next day while the women organized the baby stuff.

As they pulled out of the drive, Alyssa turned and asked why Marshall hadn't showed up.

"I have no idea. I don't see his car at the house either. I guess I should go to the house and see if he left a message on the recorder. If not, I'll call Trevor and see if he's still there," Amy said as she headed for her house.

When she got home there was no message on her answering machine. She called Trevor to see if Marshall was there.

"Trevor, it's Amy. Marshall hasn't come home. Is he still there with you?"

"No. He left a couple of hours ago."

"Oh. I wonder where he went? He was supposed to join us at a shower for one of his friends. I guess I'll go see if I can find him. I'll talk to you later. Bye."

She hung up and called her mother.

"Mom, Marshall left Trevor's a couple of hours ago. I'm going to go look for him."

"I hope nothing's wrong. I'll tell Alyssa and Dillon we'll call when we find him," Sarah said.

Amy hung up and grabbed her purse and cell phone. She left a note for Marshall to call her if he got home before she did. She wished she had gotten Marshall a cell phone for emergencies, especially now that he was driving. She drove around to his friends houses but didn't see his car anywhere. After about an hour and a half, her cell phone finally rang. Caller ID indicated that the call was from her home.

"Amy, it's Trevor," he said when she answered.

"Trevor? What are you doing at my house?"

"I found Marshall and brought him home."

"Oh. Where's his car? Is he okay?"

"His car's still at his friend's house. And he may have a touch of the alcohol flu."

"Alcohol flu? What's that?"

"You don't know much about drinking do you?"

"Drinking? Are you saying Marshall's been drinking?"

"In a round about way."

"I'll be home in a few minutes."

Amy could not imagine why Marshall would have been drinking. Perhaps Trevor was mistaken. When she pulled up in the driveway, Trevor's car was there but Marshall's wasn't. When she came into the house, she could hear the unmistakable sounds of someone with the dry heaves. She found Marshall bent over the toilet and Trevor standing at the bathroom door.

"Oh my God. I cannot believe this. Has he really been drinking?"

"Afraid so. He'll live but he's going to be sick for a while. I only had a couple of drinking experiences and they all ended this way. Alcohol and I do not mix. And it hasn't mixed well with Marshall."

Catching his breath, Marshall leaned back. He saw his mother standing at the door. He rolled back, sitting with his feet on the floor in front of him and his back to the bathtub. His face looked pale and strained.

"Sorry Mom," he said hoarsely.

"Sorry? Is that the best you can do?"

"At the moment, yes."

He slid over on his side, laying on the bathroom floor. Trevor pulled Amy away from the door and into the living room.

"I found him down the street from my house. Apparently he has a friend there and they shared some alcohol. The boy's parents are out of town and they raided the alcohol cabinet. Probably not a first for the other boy, he seemed to hold his alcohol pretty well. I saw them sitting on Marshall's car in the driveway. I stopped and talked to them and while I was there Marshall got sick. I brought him home, though we stopped a couple of times for him to throw up. We need to go get his car."

"Should we do it now? I mean, he's sick."

"He'll be fine. He'll lay on the floor for a while. I think the worse is over but he'll have a bad hangover tomorrow. I know your first instinct is to take care of him, but you're going to have to show him a little tough love. Other than the hangover, he's going to have to suffer the consequences. I don't mean to tell you how to be a parent, I've never been one, but I have been a young boy in the same exact position he's in right now. My mother was tough on me but I learned to respect her and avoid things that required her tough love."

"Okay. I've heard about tough love but right now it's tough on this parent. Let's go get his car."

Amy went to the bathroom door and Marshall looked like he had fallen asleep. She told him that they were going to get his car and he acknowledged her with a barely perceptible nod. Apparently Trevor was right, he was just going to lie there for a while. As they drove down the street, Amy was glad Sean was not home to witness his older brother's misery. And she remembered she needed to call Alyssa. Dialing on her cell phone, she hoped she did not wake Greg and Evelyn. Luckily, Dillon answered the phone.

"Dillon, this is Amy. I wanted to let Alyssa know we found Marshall and he's okay."

"Did his car break down or something?"

"Or something. It wasn't a problem with his car."

"What kind of problem was it? I won't tell Alyssa if you don't want her to know."

"I don't know if it matters, but he'd probably appreciate that. He ran into a friend that had access to some alcohol and he is currently lying on the bathroom floor. A friend of mine called it the alcohol flu."

"Oh, the alcohol flu. I've been bitten by that bug a couple of times myself. Not fun. Anything I can do?"

"I don't think so. My friend and I are getting his car. It's down the street from his house."

"Okay. I'll let Alyssa know he's okay and that he stopped by a friend's house. She'll be a little disappointed that he didn't come to the shower but she'll forgive him."

"Thanks. I'll let you know how he recovers. Bye"

As she disconnected the line, she hoped he'd recover quick because he had to work the next day. He was scheduled to go in at one o'clock so it wouldn't give him much time to get over being sick. They got to the house and the boy was still on the hood of the car, though passed out. Trevor got him up and to the door of the house. He'd probably not remember they were there come the next day. Amy drove Marshall's car back to her house and Trevor followed. She wasn't sure why he was coming back to her house or why he had even helped out but she was glad he did.

When they got back inside, Amy found that Marshall really had fallen asleep in the bathroom floor. Trevor managed to get him up and into bed. Amy was even more grateful Trevor was there to help get Marshall up because he practically had to be carried. She couldn't imagine him sleeping there all night. After getting him settled in bed, she sat on the couch and pulled her legs up under her. Trevor sat in the recliner. He looked tired and, at nearly one in the morning, she felt tired.

"Why do you think he got drunk? He's been so good through all this. He's been so grounded, so dedicated to his relationship to God, what happened for him to change and do something so stupid?"

"I don't think it's a permanent change in his character. Nothing has really changed. He's just struggling with his feelings. He's just got a lot of confused emotions right now and it's a lot to deal with. I know he looks like a young man but he's still a boy. He'll sort it out and he'll be the Christian man you know he is."

"I hope so. I thought he'd never give me any problems, he has always been so good and dependable."

"Amy. He's a boy. It's normal for boys to give their parents fits. If this is the worst you have to deal with, you are one lucky parent. He could be involved in drugs, theft, gang activity, have some girl pregnant, any number of things. If he experiments with alcohol in a confusing and difficult time, it doesn't mean he'll turn into an alcoholic on you. I think he's a normal boy trying to sort out who he is and what he's about. He'll be fine."

Amy thought about what Trevor said. She knew he was right. She had seen some kids that got involved in the wrong things, ran away from home, got in trouble with the law or ended up dead as a result of the choices they made. While both her boys may have not been perfect, they were a long way from being really troublesome. As she reflected on the truth of Trevor's statement, she drifted off to sleep curled up on the couch. She was awaken several hours later with Marshall whispering in her ear.

"Mom? Where's the aspirin?" he said quietly.

"Aspirin? It's in the bathroom cabinet. Why?" she said struggling to sit up and wondering why she was sleeping on the couch.

"My head is pounding," he replied, again in a quiet whisper.

It came back to her then. She remembered Marshall's late night adventure. She got up to get the aspirin. He waited in the living room. As she returned with a couple of tablets, he sat with his eyes closed and his face etched with pain.

"Other than having a headache, how do you feel?"

"Sick. Really sick. I guess I need to call Lydia and see if I can skip coming in this afternoon."

"Why? Why don't you plan on going to work?"

"Mom. I'm sick, that's why."

"You're not sick. You have a hangover. You made a bad decision last night. But that's not going to stop you from going to work. If you want to indulge in stupidity, you'll have to learn that there are consequences to be dealt with while you continue to take care of your business."

"Are you saying I can't call in sick?"

"Yes, because you're not sick. You should have known better than to do something like that. And while we are on the subject, why did you do it?"

"I don't know. Zach asked me if I wanted a drink and I accepted. I didn't intend to get drunk or anything."

"But why did you accept it?"

"I just did. You know I'm not perfect. You can't expect me to never make a mistake."

"A mistake is doing something you didn't intend to do. It's an accident. It may have been an accident that you got drunk and ended up with a hangover but it was no accident when you took that drink. You took it knowing what you were doing. You made a conscious choice to drink when you knew you shouldn't."

"Dad did drugs. At least I didn't get high."

"That's a poor attempt to rationalize your actions. You are not like your father. You saw what his actions lead to. You are a Christian and you know better than to make the same choices. And as a Christian, you have a higher accountability before God."

"How do you know I'm not like my father? How do you know that I won't end up like him, beating up my wife and abusing my kids? How do you know I'm any different than he was?"

"Is that what you want to do, to be like? It's your choice. It's dependent on what path you choose to take."

"No, it's not what I want to be like. But how do I know I won't? Dad didn't want to be like that either. He wanted to be a better person but he didn't know how. He got involved in drugs and didn't know how to get out. He lost respect for himself and couldn't face you."

"How do you know what he felt?"

"He told me once. He said he'd done a lot of things he was ashamed of and you made him feel bad because you were so good and pure. He couldn't deal with the way it made him feel so he just did more drugs and hung out with women who didn't make him feel bad."

"He told you that? When did you have this conversation?"

"It was right before he left. You had went to the store with Sean and I was in my room. He came in and just started talking to me. I wanted him to leave but he just kept talking. I hated him for what he had done to us and I didn't want to hear what he had to say. I thought it was stupid. He said one day I'd be a man and would understand what he was saying. I asked him why he married you if you made him feel bad about himself. He said he thought it would make him a better person but it didn't, it just made him feel worse about himself. I had a hard time facing him after that. I tried to love him like you wanted but I just couldn't. I didn't want to see him in the hospital. But I didn't think he was going to die. I'm sorry Mom, I failed you and God."

Marshall's voice broke and he put his head in his hands. Amy sat beside him and stroked his back

"Son, you didn't fail me. And you didn't fail God. He understands what you were feeling. But you have to come to terms with your feelings about your father. As difficult as it may be you will have to forgive him for what he did and find some love in your heart for him. Remember that conversation you had with Sean about loving people even though they made mistakes in their lives? You were talking about Lacy but it applies to your father as well."

"I know. It's easier to say you love someone than actually loving them. And Lacy is easier to love than Dad was. And it's easier to say you want to do the right things than actually doing them."

"I know. It's not a problem unique to us. Paul struggled with the same issues. Remember? He was a great minister of the gospel, starting new churches, teaching new converts. He was one of the greatest teachers in the New Testament and he said he had trouble doing what was right even when he wanted to do it. Paul said although he delighted in serving God, a war waged inside him between good and evil. He called himself a wretched man because of his lack of control over his sinful nature.

"He seemed to do the wrong thing when in his heart he meant to do the right thing. He said that only God, through Jesus, could save him from his sinful nature. We have to renew our mind, which transforms our nature and helps us to live according to God's will and not our own. If he struggled with it, why do you think we'd have an easier time?"

Marshall looked up at her. He sat up and wrapped his arms around her in a tight hug.

"I had forgotten about that. I guess we're all human, even Paul. Thanks Mom. Thanks for helping me understand. I'm sorry about last night. If you don't mind, I think I'll sleep for a little bit before getting up and going to work. But I need you to take me to get my car."

"I've already gotten your car. Remember? Trevor and I went and got it last night."

"Oh. Last night is a bit confused in my head. I seem to remember him being here."

"I'm still here," Trevor said at the doorway. "Your mom fell asleep on the couch and I didn't think I could make it home in one piece so I slept in the other bedroom. I hope that's alright."

Amy looked up at Trevor. She hadn't realized he was still at the house.

"That's fine. I didn't realize you were here, though I didn't remember you leaving either. Sorry I went to sleep on you."

"Not a problem. But I guess I should head for home. Call me if you need me. And Marshall, I still want you to go with me to the Homework House this coming week. I'll call you later."

"Sure. See you then. And thanks for helping my mom last night," Marshall said as he headed for his room to sleep off the last of his hangover.

Chapter Twenty-One

A my was getting ready to close the office when her cell phone rang. As she punched in the alarm code, she answered the phone.

"Hello."

"Amy, it's James. Got any plans this evening?"

"Uh, no. Except to fix dinner for Sean. Marshall is helping a friend this afternoon so it'll be just the two of us."

"Well, it sounds like a boring evening. How about me livening it up for you? Lacy is in labor and we're heading for the hospital. She wanted me to call you. I've already spoken to Sarah and she and Sean are coming to the hospital."

"In labor? How's she doing?"

"She's doing pretty good. Better than I thought she would, actually."

"Well, I'm going to run by the house and change clothes and then I'll met you there."

"Okay, see you there."

Amy made a mad dash home and put on a comfortable shirt and jeans. She called Trevor's cell number and left a message for him to pass on to Marshall. The two of them were at Homework House. Marshall had gotten a day off so he could go as he had promised. She hoped it would be a good experience for him. She pulled into the hospital parking lot and ran to the emergency room door. She was directed to the delivery room waiting area. Sean and Sarah were there along with James, Stevie and baby Matthew.

"Where's Kim," Amy asked.

"She's in the labor room with Lacy," James answered.

"Oh. Is Karen not going to come be with Lacy?"

"Um, no."

James motioned for her to follow him out of the room. She wondered what was up.

"Karen has problems of her own," he said leading her away from the door. "She's here in the hospital. She tried to commit suicide."

"What? Why?" Amy stammered.

"It seems her boyfriend took everything he could from her and split. She was more upset over his leaving than his cleaning her out. She took a handful of pills and washed them down with whiskey. She's physically okay but seems emotionally unbalanced."

"Does Lacy know?"

"Yeah. Karen called her for some reason and told her what Neal had done. She had already taken the pills when she called. Lacy told me and I called the police. She said Karen sounded hateful on the phone like it was all her fault but she didn't understand why she would, she hadn't even been there. I talked to Karen after they brought her in and she said Neal told her he would rather have her daughter than a used up old woman like her. Even though he cleaned her out and said what he did, Karen said she doesn't want to press charges just in case he changes his mind and wants her back."

"That's crazy. Stevie doesn't know, does he, that his mom tried to kill herself?"

"No. He'd never understand. He doesn't understand why his mother doesn't want him with her. I know this will all probably come out someday but I'd rather it be when he's old enough to handle it."

"Yeah, that'd be best. Thanks for telling me."

James headed back to the waiting room. Amy went to the front of the hospital to make a phone call.

"Hello," Evelyn answered.

"Hello, Evelyn. It's Amy. Is Alyssa home?"

"Sure. Let me get her for you."

"Hi Amy," Alyssa said as she answered.

"Hey sweetie. I just wanted to let you know Lacy is in labor and we're at the hospital."

"It's time? Is she okay?"

"James said she's doing really good. I don't know how long it'll be before the baby comes but I wanted to let you and Dillon know."

"Thanks. He's not home from work yet but as soon as he comes in we'll come to the hospital. Tell her to wait until we get there," Alyssa said laughing.

"I'll tell her but it's up to the baby when he decides to make his appearance."

Amy hung up the phone with a smile on her face. She headed to the waiting room to check on Lacy. James told her a nurse had come out and said it would probably be several more hours before the baby was delivered. He said that he had ordered some pizza and was going to pick it up. Both the boys wanted to ride with him since Matthew was going. After they left, Amy decided to continue an earlier conversation she had had with her mother.

"Mom, remember when you came to the house and told me you were getting married? You said we'd continue our conversation later? I'd like to do that now. But I have a question for you, something I've been wondering about. When Kevin and I were growing up, I don't remember you.....you know, being real...umm....affectionate. I don't mean that you didn't love us but I don't remember you hugging us or anything. But I see you do that with mine and Kevin's kids."

Sarah sighed. "No, I didn't. I wanted to but I was afraid to. I loved all over you when you were a baby. But after Curtis told me he didn't love me, something inside me just dammed up. I felt like if I loved on you, I would lose you. I was afraid, I guess, that if I loved you too much you'd push me away. I couldn't handle being pushed away by my own children. I felt unlovable. It was silly, I had no reason to feel that way."

"What changed to make you able to love your grandkids?"

"I don't really know. I remember when Katie was born, I watched Kevin kiss her face and hands and feet. He was just bursting with love for his baby girl. He handed her to me and I just looked at her. I didn't know what to do. Kevin put his arm around my shoulders and pulled her and me into an embrace. I realized that my son loved me and I could love him back. I could love his daughter all I wanted to. I pulled her close and kissed her forehead and the dam broke. Then I felt like I just couldn't love people enough. When Marshall was born, I felt like he was my child. I wanted to feel all that I had missed with my own babies. I missed so much with you and Kevin because of an irrational fear. I have tried to make it up to you and your brother. I hope you can forgive me."

"Mom. You don't have to make anything up with us. We love you. You were a good mother. We learned so much from you. You were strong and resilient; you had courage. You lived what you taught us. You didn't say one thing and do another. You gave us morals and convictions. You taught us about God and showed us how to live for him through the way you lived. And you're the best grandmother my children could ever have."

Amy and Sarah were in tears when James came back with the boys and the pizza. As they were having a greasy supper in the waiting room, Alyssa and Dillon joined them. A short while later Loren and Marshall joined the party. The nurse appeared ever so often to say everything was going well with Lacy and the baby. After several hours, Sean and Stevie were nearly as cranky as Matthew. Finally the nurse appeared to announce the baby was on his way. Moments later the hearty cries of the newborn could be heard. Everyone trooped to the nursery window for the first peak of the Selby addition.

He was brought to the window and everyone watched as he was weighed and measured. The boys thought he was funny, wiggling and crying as the nurses poked and prodded him. Kim came out and asked for James and Amy to come to the delivery room. They found an exuberant new mother waiting for them.

"Did you see him? Isn't he beautiful?"

"We did and he is. Congratulations," Amy said as she hugged Lacy.

"Well, Mom. How do you feel?" James asked his daughter.

"Weird. I have a baby. It's just so awesome. I mean I came here with the baby inside me and now he's outside. That little baby was inside me. It's just so incredible."

"Pretty spectacular. Child birth is the greatest miracle. It never ceases to amaze me," Amy said.

"They're going to put me in a room and then bring the baby to me to try and feed. The doctor said if everything goes okay, I'll go home tomorrow."

"I'm sure everything will be just fine," Amy assured her.

"Who's all here?" Lacy asked.

"Sarah, Loren, Marshall, all three boys, Alyssa and Dillon. I'm glad you finally delivered the baby. Stevie, Sean

177

and Matthew were getting restless, not to mention the rest of us. Did everything go okay?" James asked.

"I guess so. The nurse said things were progressing like they were supposed to, whatever that means. But I feel fine. I just want to see my baby."

"We keep calling him the baby. Have you settled on a name?" James asked.

"He's Dustin James Selby. D.J. I thought about different names but kept coming back to that one. It sounds right," Lacy said with tenderness in her eyes as she looked at her father.

"I like it," he said as he stroked her cheek.

The nurse came in and said they were ready to move her to a private room. Lacy scooted out of the bed and into a wheel chair. The nurse rolled her down the hall into another room. Lacy winced as she crawled into the bed. As soon as she was settled, the room filled with her guests. Dillon had a vase of flowers for her and Alyssa gave her a little blue teddy bear. Marshall handed her a gift basket filled with chocolate. Stevie and Sean had a bouquet of balloons they wrestled from Matthew to hand her. Lacy was so happy she began to cry. The nurse appeared with D.J. and handed him to his mother. Lacy held him close and rubbed her lips over his face. She then handed him to her father.

"Here you go gramps," she said with a smile.

"Gramps, huh? I can deal with that," James said.

"I want to hold him, he's my brother," Stevie said.

"He's not your brother," Kim corrected him. "He's your nephew."

"What's that?" he asked.

"You're his uncle," Dillon explained.

"He's my brother. Matthew is a baby and I'm his brother. Besides, I'm not old enough to be an uncle," Stevie reasoned.

"You can be an uncle no matter what age you are. Matthew is D.J.'s uncle too," James told him.

"Who's D.J." Sean asked.

"The baby is D.J.," Marshall answered.

While the conversation went on, Lacy began to fall asleep. The nurse came in and ushered the visitors out the door so Lacy could feed the baby before she went to sleep. She told them visiting hours were over and they could come back in the morning. The little group dispersed, all nearly as tired as the new mother. Amy drove home and had to wake Sean up to get him in the house. She asked Marshall how things had gone at Homework House.

"I liked it. I didn't think I would though. There was one little boy there, Kendrick, that was so timid. I worked with him on the computer, showing him how to use it. Every time I moved my hand he flinched like I was going to hit him. After about a hour he loosened up and was real eager to learn. I didn't realize that there were some kids that had no opportunities to do things we take for granted. It seemed like Kendrick never had anyone do anything nice for him. If I told him he did a good job, he acted like he was going to cry with joy. I felt sorry for him.

"Trevor said the kids need mentors, like Big Brothers and Big Sisters. I saw the difference it makes for someone to show a little interest in them. I told Trevor I wanted to help more often, especially with Kendrick. Trevor said Kendrick's mother is in prison for selling drugs and he lives with his grandparents. His grandfather is mean to him, at least that's what he told me. I can get out of school early on Tuesdays so I think I'll go to the elementary school and visit him in his class. Trevor said he does that with one little boy. It makes the kids feel special he said."

Amy was surprised that he was so excited about helping underprivileged kids. But she was glad he had chosen to get involved. As Marshall went to his room, she thought there was a time she would have thought her own kids were underprivileged. But they were very blessed. They didn't have to worry about what they would eat, or if they would eat. They had a nice home, plenty of food and a close, loving and nurturing family. She went to bed with a happy heart.

The next day Lacy and D.J. came home. Before Amy went to visit them, she went to the hospital. She wanted to see Karen. She found her curled in the bed and extremely despondent.

"Karen. How are you doing?" Amy asked.

"I want to die," came the pitiful answer.

"No you don't. Your life isn't over," Amy insisted.

"You don't know what you're talking about. What is there to live for?"

"What about your children? What about yourself?"

"My children are fine. I don't want to live without Neal."

"Neal used you. He took advantage of you. Why would you want to be with him?"

"I love him. He's all I want."

"Karen. You'll meet someone else that will really love you."

"I don't want someone else. I want Neal. I want to die."

"You need to be strong and move on. Let him go."

"I don't want to let him go. I'm not strong enough to move on without him."

"God can give you the strength if you'll let him."

"I don't want any part of your God. He hasn't done anything for me. Go away and leave me alone."

Karen was angry and Amy thought it best to comply with her wishes. She left though saddened by Karen's attitude. She hoped the doctors could help her get straightened out. It would be a shame if she was successful in taking her life. Amy drove to Lacy's house and was glad James had taken his children to live with him. There was no telling what would have happened to them if they had been at home with their mother when she took the pills.

Chapter Twenty-Two

Amy was standing in the living room gently rocking D.J. He had proved to be a good tempered baby. Lacy had gotten him on a schedule for eating and sleeping that allowed her to go to school without being worn out. Kim was a great help and the two of them shared keeping the little ones so neither got burned out. Amy was glad to see they had worked everything out between them and had developed a good relationship. She saw it as hope that mixed families could make it. Though she wasn't absolutely certain why that mattered to her. Except that thoughts about Trevor kept creeping into her mind. She tried to banish them, tried to tell herself she wasn't interested in him except as a friend. And she was sure he had no interest in her except as a friend. Surely he would prefer a woman to have his own family with, not a ready made family. But with all the rationalizing she did in her mind, her thoughts kept coming back to him.

She sighed and shook her head. D.J. wiggled and made the little sucking motion with his mouth so common to all babies. It brought back memories of her own babies. As she watched the infant sleep in her arms, she felt such overwhelming peace flow over her. She reflected on the past months. She and the boys had come a long way, traveled through a storm she could never have imagined. And they had come through it stronger and wiser. She remembered being so low, feeling nearly hopeless, overcome with despair. And then it seemed as if God had reached down and touched her, giving her strength to push on and go forward.

She remembered a scene in a movie where the heroine had fought her way through battering rain and wind, struggled over rocky terrain, persevering despite the odds. When she finally reached shelter, she was bruised and bloody but safe. It was what Amy felt. Safe. She knew her strength was from God. There was no way she could have made it through without his help and his injection of peace when she needed it.

She had been reading in Romans and several scriptures seemed to sum things up for her.

"We have peace with God through our Lord Jesus Christ, through whom we have gained access by faith into this grace which we now stand. And we rejoice in the hope of the glory of God. Not only so, but we also rejoice in our sufferings, because we know that suffering produces perseverance; perseverance, character; and character hope. And hope does not disappoint us," the scriptures said.

While she had suffered, at least that was the way she saw it, she had gained strength, character and hope. The result was peace. Her life had changed so much since she had walked out of the courthouse that afternoon months past. She was more aware of what was important in life and how to deal with what wasn't. She believed both her sons had learned a few things too. And she had a great appreciation for others who had similar experiences. She had not realized her own mother had went through many of the same things she had. And she had created bonds with several new friends. She looked at the baby she held and felt she had received a great gift of friendship from his mother and her family.

The ringing of the doorbell made both her and the baby jump. Peering through the peep hole she saw Trevor standing there. She carefully opened the door so she wouldn't disturb the baby.

"Hey," she said quietly.

"Hey. Who's baby?" he asked.

"A young friend of mine's. She's with the other kids from church at a youth convention."

"Kid? This little one's mother is a kid?"

"Yep. Sixteen. But she's been a great mother. I told her I'd watch the baby while she went to the convention. Her mother is in the hospital and her dad and step mom are taking a break for their anniversary. Besides they have a two year old of their own."

"How old is this little one? Boy or girl?"

"Boy. He's three weeks. His name is D.J."

"Oh, this must be the baby you called about when Marshall and I were at the Homework House. Can I hold him or will it wake him up?"

"He's a pretty heavy sleeper. Here," she said as she handed him the baby.

She showed him how to support the baby's head. He looked comfortable holding the infant.

"My brother had a little girl. Well, his girlfriend does. She's four. He died before she was born. I don't even think he knew his girlfriend was pregnant. I've seen her several times and she's so beautiful. She looks like her mother, thank goodness. I've talked to her mom and we've worked it out so when Kyla is old enough she can come spend some time with me. She can get to know our family. My parents see her but they don't think they can take care of her by themselves," Trevor said.

"I'd think four is old enough to get to know her uncle. She does know who you are, doesn't she?" Amy asked.

"Yeah, as much as a four year old can. I don't know how my brother found such a good woman with all he was mixed up in but he did. She's going back to school so she can provide a good life for Kyla. I help out some each month so Kyla can attend a good daycare."

"Do you want to have kids of your own? You seem to be so good with them. You knew how to handle Marshall. You work with the kids at the Homework House. You are developing a relationship with your niece."

"I've though about it. At my age, I'd have to rob the cradle practically to get someone young enough to have a baby. Most women my age have already had families. I'd like to be a dad but it would most likely be as a step-dad. I don't have a problem with that. My parents want me to get married and have kids. I've got to find a woman willing to have me before I can get married. And I think I'm a bit old to begin having babies."

"Oh, I don't think you'd have a hard time finding a woman of any age that would be glad to have you. You look like you could handle mowing the yard, killing bugs and changing flat tires."

"You think that's all a man's good for? I'll have you know I can cook a mean pot roast, bleach the whites and make a bed."

"Well, you are quite a catch then," Amy teased.

The baby began to stir, stretching and grunting. He opened his eyes and began whimpering. Amy took him and changed his diaper. She handed him back to Trevor and went to the kitchen to fix him a bottle. Trevor took the bottle and fed the baby like a pro.

"This isn't so hard. Why do men complain about taking care of babies?" Trevor asked. No sooner had the words come from his mouth when D.J. grunted and an unmistakable odor filled the room.

"Oh. I remember now," he said, scrunching his face up.

Amy got up to take the baby. Trevor handed her the bottle.

"I'll do it. I'm a tough man, I can handle a little baby poo," he said.

Amy handed him a diaper, baby wipes and a diaper pad. He laid the baby on the floor and tugged open his sleeper. When he pulled the tabs on the diaper, he began to look uncertain. Amy watched as he lifted the baby's bottom and began to clean the baby up. She took the dirty diaper to the garbage in the garage and when she came back Trevor was trying to get the diaper on the baby backwards. She laughed and turned the diaper around. He finally got the baby diapered and struggled to get his feet back into his sleeper.

"Women make it look easier than it is. But you have to admit that for a first time, I did pretty good."

"You did very good. But I want to see you do it when the baby is nine months old and crawling away."

"That sounds like a challenge. I'm going to take you up on that."

He picked the baby up and gave him his bottle. After a while the baby drifted back to sleep and Amy put him on her bed.

"Could I interest you in dinner?" Trevor asked when she returned to the living room.

"What do you have in mind?" she replied.

"How about some Chinese carryout?"

"I love Chinese. But are you sure? Surely you have something better to do than sit around with me as I baby sit."

"I'm sure. I enjoy your company. When are the kids coming back?"

"Marshall and his group will be in around eleven. Lacy's dad is picking up the baby around nine so he can be put down for the night in his own bed. Sean is spending the night with Sylvia. Why?"

"Well, I'd hate to bring food in and not have enough to go around."

Trevor called in to place an order. When he sat back on the sofa next to Amy, he had a question in his eyes.

"Amy, I've seen people go through much less than you have and fall apart. Where do you get our strength from?"

"From God. I couldn't have handled all this without him. I stayed with Brandon because I didn't know I had any options. I was afraid I couldn't make it without his help. Then I realized I wasn't getting any help from him. I spent many nights on my knees crying to God for help. I didn't think I was making any progress. I felt like I was at the end of my rope and losing my grip. I though each new problem would be the one to swamp me. But I realize now that I was getting stronger instead of weaker. God sustained me through each situation. I'm sure there are things I still have to go through but I know he'll go through them with me. He gives me peace in the storm."

"Peace. What a great feeling. I thought you were a Christian when I first met you. You had look about you."

"What look?"

"That look of assurance, peace. It was all over your face, even with Colette screaming at you. I was intrigued by you. I wanted to get to know you."

"What about you? Are you a Christian?"

"Absolutely. I haven't always been. I mean I was raised in church but didn't take it seriously. After my brother got killed I began taking stock of my life. I figured it was time to get in touch with God and get everything straightened out between us. I wished I'd done it a long time ago because it is such a wonderful feeling. I guess it's time to go get our food. I'll be right back."

Trevor left and the house seemed suddenly quiet. Amy went in to check on the baby. He was still asleep. As she headed back to the living room the phone rang. She grabbed it before it woke D.J.

"Hello."

"Mom, I just wanted to let you know after the service tonight we're all going to go get something to eat. It'll probably be late before I get in. I didn't want you to worry," Marshall said.

"Okay. I'm glad you called and let me know. How's the convention?"

"It's great. I'm so glad I came. I really needed this. Even Dillon is getting into the Spirit. I've got to run. Don't stay up for me. I love you. Bye."

Amy hung up the phone. She wondered how many boys would tell their mother they loved them in a crowd of their peers. After a while she heard a car pull into the driveway. Opening the door she found James standing there instead of Trevor.

"Hey, it's not nine o'clock yet," she said.

"I know. My sister showed up at my house and wants to see the baby. I didn't know she was coming in or I would of made other plans. I'm going to take the runt off your hands and appease my sister."

Amy lead him into the house and watched as he scooped up his grandchild.

"You know, I really thought that things would have been much worse than they are. Lacy has been a good parent and has been a real help around the house. She and Kim get along well. It's really not a bad situation. I want to thank you for being so kind to her and being her friend."

"It's been my pleasure really. She's kind of become like my daughter. I guess this is preparation for when I become a grandmother, though I hope it doesn't happen soon."

She waved him off. As he was pulling out of the driveway, Trevor was pulling in.

"Who was that?" he asked.

"D.J.'s grandpa. He took him home early. Come on in, that food smells so good."

Amy spread the table and they dug in. It had been a while since Amy had Chinese food and she relished every bite. Once the meal was over they put away the leftovers and cleaned off the table. Amy felt very comfortable with Trevor. They talked about silly things and laughed together. As Trevor was preparing to leave for the night, he turned serious.

"I want to thank you for a wonderful evening. I don't remember when I had such a nice time," he said.

"That's hard to believe. We didn't do anything special."

"It was the company that made it great."

Trevor stroked Amy's cheek. Her heart began to pound. She was nearly breathless when he gently kissed her. She felt like she had been kissed for the first time. She suddenly felt like she was sixteen again, shot through with wild emotions.

"I'll see you later," he said as he backed up to the door.

She followed, drawn to him. "Okay," was all she could say.

He bumped his way out the door. She stood in the doorway, watching him leave. She had no idea she could feel this way. As she closed and locked the door, she wanted to run through the house dancing and yelling like a kid. She managed to maintain her dignity all the way to the phone. Dialing Lydia's number, she had started to giggle.

"Lydia, you won't believe this," she said when Lydia answered.

"What? Are you okay?" Lydia asked.

"I'm great."

"So tell me about it."

"I've just been kissed."

"What? Have you been holding out on me? Spill it. No, wait. I've got ice cream and I'm on my way."

Amy was nearly giddy when she hung up the phone.

"God, you sure know what you're doing. You've brought me through the storm and into the sunshine on the other side. Thank you, thank you, thank you," she said as she danced into the kitchen for a couple of spoons.

.

About The Author

Deirdre Kelley works as a news paper reporter in Southeast Arkansas. She has returned to school to further her education, seeking a degree in Journalism and English the Houston native became a single parent early on raising three loving boys to manhood. She attributes her strength and perseverance, over coming great odds, to her faith in God.

Printed in the United States
123711LV00001B/28/A

9 781420 829808